Jacob of Sarug's Homily on Epiphany

TEXTS FROM CHRISTIAN LATE ANTIQUITY

4

General Editor
George A. Kiraz

The Metrical Homilies of Mar Jacob of Sarug

GENERAL EDITOR
SEBASTIAN P. BROCK

MANAGING EDITOR
GEORGE A. KIRAZ

FASCICLE 2

JACOB OF SARUG'S HOMILY ON EPIPHANY

TRANSLATED WITH INTRODUCTION BY
THOMAS KOLLAMPARAMPIL

GORGIAS PRESS
2008

First Gorgias Press Edition, 2008

Copyright © 2008 by Gorgias Press LLC

All rights reserved under International and Pan-American Copyright Conventions. No part of this publication may be reproduced, stored in a retrieval system or transmitted in any form or by any means, electronic, mechanical, photocopying, recording, scanning or otherwise without the prior written permission of Gorgias Press LLC.

Published in the United States of America by Gorgias Press LLC, New Jersey

ISBN 978-1-59333-736-0
ISSN 1935-6846

GORGIAS PRESS
180 Centennial Ave., Suite 3, Piscataway, NJ 08854 USA
www.gorgiaspress.com

Library of Congress Cataloging-in-Publication Data
Jacob, of Serug, 451-521.
 [Homily on Epiphany. English & Syriac]
 Jacob of Sarug's Homily on Epiphany / translated with introduction by Thomas Kollamparampil. -- 1st Gorgias Press ed.
   p. cm. -- (Texts from Christian late antiquity ; 4) (Metrical homilies of Mar Jacob of Sarug ; fasc. 2)
 Includes index.
 1. Epiphany--Sermons. 2. Sermons, Syriac. 3. Sermons, Syriac--Translations into English. I. Kollamparampil, Thomas. II. Title. III. Title: Homily on Epiphany.
 BV50.E7J3313 2008
 252'.615--dc22
                                                2008008885

The paper used in this publication meets the minimum requirements of the American National Standards.

Printed in the United States of America

This publication was made possible with a generous grant from

The Barnabas Fund

and

The Athanasius Yeshu Samuel Fund

TABLE OF CONTENTS

Table of Contents v
List of Abbreviations vii
Introduction 1
    Outline 1
    Summary 3
Text and Translation 5
    The Betrothal of the Bridegroom to the Bride, the Church 6
    John the Baptist, the Adorner of the Bride 8
    Isaiah, the Instructor of the Bride 10
    John the Baptist, the Trustworthy of the Bride 12
    The True Bridegroom awaited by the Church and John the Baptist ... 14
    John the Baptist's Expectation for the Mighty Voice of the Father 16
    The Ornate Bride and the Wedding-Guests Expecting 'the White Garment' 20
    The Arrival of the Bridegroom for Baptism 22
    The Bride Instructed by John the Baptist and David 24
    John's Refusal to Baptize Christ 28
    Christ's Demand for Baptism for the Recovery of Adam 30
    John's Confession of His Inability before the Royal Son 32
    The Reason and Righteousness of Christ's Descent for Baptism 36
    The Apparent Impossibility For John to Baptize 'the Baptizer of All' 40
    The Son's Command to John and the Baptism of the Holy One 44
    The Baptism of the Son and the Sanctification of the Waters 44
    The Father and the Holy Spirit Bearing Witness upon the Son 48
    The Bride's Recognition of the Royal Bridegroom 52
    The Baptism of Jesus and the Proclamation of the Father 56
    The Flowing of Priesthood, Kingship and Holiness into Christ 62
Bibliography of Works Cited 69
    (a) Syriac authors 69
    (b) Modern works 70

Index of Names and Themes 71
Index of Biblical References 72

List of Abbreviations

Bedjan	P. Bedjan, *Homiliae Selectae Mar-Jacobi Sarugensis* (see BIBLIOGRAPHY)
CSCO	Corpus Scriptorum Christianorum Orientalium
OCA	Orientalia Christiana Analecta
OrSyr	*L'Orient Syrien*
PO	Patrologia Orientalis

INTRODUCTION

> INFORMATION ON THIS HOMILY
> Homily Title: On the Baptism of Our Redeemer in the Jordan
> Source of Text: *Homiliae selectae Mar-Jacobi Sarugensis* edited by Paul Bedjan (Paris-Leipzig 1905, 2nd ed. Piscataway: Gorgias Press, 2006), vol. 1, pp. 167–193. [Homily 8]
> Lines: 532

OUTLINE

The world became aware of the betrothal of Christ to the Church of the nations. Christ, the Bridegroom, is not unaware of the persecuted and afflicted Church that had become immersed in idolatry by defiling herself. So she should be sent down to the waters that had been prepared to wash and to brighten her colour that has been altered by the incense to the idols. Hence, 'the robe of glory' has been placed in the womb of baptism and the bride is sent down to clothe herself from the waters (1–16). John the Baptist was sent to carry the adornment and to clothe the bride with sanctity. The bride understood John from the instructions of Isaiah regarding the one calling out in the wilderness. Hence John became trusted by the bride even to the point of her supposing him to be her Bridegroom because the Messiah was still concealed. But the faithful servant, John the Baptist, hurriedly cut off this stumbling block. He declared that he was not the Bridegroom who is older than him. He instructed her to look ahead for the coming of her Bridegroom. The Church, the bride, gathered herself around John in the desert, waiting for the Bridegroom in order to enter with him into the womb of the waters so as to be sanctified. John had expected to see his own baptism made perfect through that of Christ (17–90).

All 'wedding guests' were cleansed and the bride was made perfect with the washing. Yet none has received the garments of the Spirit from the water and that baptism remained deficient of forgiveness. Then the royal Son came out from the crowds. The Holy Spirit came out by itself and stood above the water and kindled it. The river exulted and the baptismal water became heated up as the horn of anointing in response to David (cf. 1 Sam 16:1–13). It was not to render sanctification to the Son, the Holy One, but so that the Son might sanctify the womb of baptismal waters. John having understood that the Holy One had come to baptism, drew back from baptizing so that Christ, the Bridegroom, might alone stand out as the sacrificial lamb that might go out from the flock (cf. Lev 16:20–31). John, the faithful servant, showed the bride who her Lord is. He declared that she was from the beginning betrothed to this Bridegroom and that he himself guarded her with watchful care. The Bridegroom himself came like the lamb who carries away the sin of the world. David too assures the bride regarding her Lord and advises her not to waver but to hear and adore him (93–180).

John refused to baptize the Holy One, believing that he himself had to be baptized by Christ. The true Governor is Christ and John had only kept the office for him. John established his argument saying that Christ lacks nothing and hence there is nothing to be gained from baptism because propitiation, forgiveness, priesthood, kingship and holiness are all in the Son, the fullness of divinity (181–200). Jesus replied that the real need is for the recovery of Adam, the fair image. The search for Adam who by his own will perished at the hands of the evil one, has brought Jesus to effect this. Adam wanted to enter into his inheritance, but fell and wasted away. But the Loving Kindness that called Christ to come to birth has again called him to come to baptism. Now Christ has to perfect the road upon which he has come (201–236).

John confessed his inability and admitted his lowly state before Christ. John believed that Christ needed no armour from the water and requested the Royal Son to proceed to deliver the captives from the captors (237–264). Jesus appraised John that actually waters needed sanctification and his descent was not to take any shield from the water but as the Commander he would set up a mighty armour for the warriors. Since humanity needs to equip itself with the power of Christ from the waters, Christ himself enters into the 'Furnace of water' to recast humanity and the 'Tomb of water' to make humanity immortal in the resurrection (265–290). John had told the bride that her Lord would baptize with the Holy Spirit and fire, and that he himself is not worthy even for the sandals of the Bridegroom. Hence, if he baptizes Christ the bride will find John to be false and Christ, her Bridegroom, to be deficient. Moreover, in whose name would John baptize the Baptizer of all, who is there together with his Father and the Holy Spirit in an undivided harmony (291–318). The Son commanded John to suspend all disputations and to place the hand upon his head in silence. It is the prerogative of the Father to declare about the Son and that of the Spirit to bear witness (319–326). As the Holy One reached the waters the river leaped for joy in the pure womb of baptism just as John in the womb of Elizabeth towards his Lord. The Living Fire came down and kindled the river in holiness and the Fiery Coal descended for washing and sprinkled its fieriness of holiness (331–354).

The Spirit was there to receive the Son in splendour. The clouds issued forth and constructed a bridal chamber for the glorious Bridegroom. The Father rent the sky and raised his voice saying, "Behold, this is my Son; this is truly my Beloved." The Spirit came there not to sanctify the Son but to act as a 'finger to the Father' and thus the Father pointed out who his Beloved is. The Law too calls for two witnesses, and the Father and the Spirit together bore witness to the Son (355–400).

The bride, the Church, marvelled at the Royal Bridegroom because in his baptism the height and the depth were reconciled. David, the Harp of the Spirit, was called to sing out songs of glory as well as to explain the signs that happened. The words of David, "The waters have seen you, God and they feared" (Ps 77:16), explained the fact and proclaimed that the whole nature of waters became stirred by his descent. Zechariah too came and showed that this was the One whose name is "Day-Star" *(denḥa)*. The Father himself, unlike other times, without any intermediary, spoke from his essence to indicate that truly his Son was there, for he does not have any other Son (401–496).

The Father gave the deposit of everything, Priesthood, Kingdom and Holiness, to Moses on the mountain. The tribe of Levi handed it down. The Lion's Whelp of Judah arose and took it up from John. The Aaronic priesthood then proceeded from the Redeemer through the apostles to the world. As water by nature flows to the sea, so also what belonged to Christ naturally came to him. From what was originally established by the Father and belonged to Christ, the Son made a renewal of the old things. The bride, the Church, recognized her Bridegroom. She fell down before him, the Perfect One, who came down to make perfect the imperfect by the water of the sanctified baptism (497–530).

Summary

The Betrothal of the Bridegroom to the Bride, the Church (1–16)
John the Baptist, the Adorner of the Bride (17–30)
Isaiah, the Instructor of the Bride (31–56)
John the Baptist, the Trustworthy of the Bride (57–74)
The True Bridegroom awaited by the Bride and John the Baptist (75–88)

John the Baptist's Expectation for the Mighty Voice of the Father (89–114)
The Ornate Bride and the Wedding-Guests Expecting 'the White Garment' (115–134)
The Arrival of the Bridegroom for Baptism (135–160)
The Bride Instructed by John the Baptist and David (161–180)
John's Refusal to Baptize Christ (181–200)
Christ's Demand for Baptism for the Recovery of Adam (201–236)
John's Confession of His Inability before the Royal Son (237–264)
The Reason and Righteousness of Christ's Descent for Baptism (265–290)
John's Apparent Impossibility to Baptize 'the Baptizer of All' (291–318)
The Son's Command to John and the Baptism of the Holy One (319–326)
The Baptism of the Son and the Sanctification of the Waters (327–354)
The Father and the Holy Spirit Bearing Witness upon the Son (355–400)
The Bride's Recognition of the Royal Bridegroom (401–444)
The Baptism of Jesus and the Proclamation of the Father (445–496)
The Flowing of Priesthood, Kingship and Holiness into Christ (497–532)

Text and Translation

The Betrothal of the Bridegroom to the Bride, the Church

1   Christ, the Bridegroom prepared the marriage feast for the church of the nations[1]   Matt 22:2–14; Luke 14:16–24

and the world became aware of the wedding feast He had furnished for her *[the Church]*.

The Royal Son wished to betroth the afflicted one *[the Church]*   Hos 2:19,20; 2 Cor 11:2

and He sent her to go to the fountain to wash away her dust.   Zech 13:1

5   He saw the persecuted (Church) that was weak, desiccated and wearied,

then He mixed waters and sent her to wash herself, and then to be betrothed.

He had regard for her beauty that was altered by the incense of idols;[2]

and He poured out rushing streams of the river upon her face to brighten her colour.[3]

He sent her down first to the tested waters[4] as He betrothed her,   Judg 7:1–4

10   in order to purge away fornication from her by sanctification.

That smell of the holocausts sacrificed was concentrated in her,[5]

---

[1] The replacing of the 'chosen people' with the 'new people' or 'the nations' of the gentiles is a predominant theme in Aphrahat and Ephrem. This is shared by Jacob of Serugh also. Cf. *Dem* XVII 7; cf. R. Murray, *Symbols of Church and Kingdom*, pp. 41–68; S. P. Brock, *The Luminous Eye*, pp. 116–122.

[2] J.-P. P. Martin, "Sur la chute des idoles," p. 112, tr. p. 133.

[3] Cf. S. P. Brock, "Baptismal Themes," p. 342 (n. 107 refers to the 'black girl' as having changed the colour due to conversion in a metaphorical sense).

[4] 'Tested waters of Gideon': cf. Albert, *Juifs*, IV 225–6; Bedjan III, p. 317; Aphrahat, *Dem* VII.18,19; S. P. Brock, "Baptismal Themes," p. 342 (ns. 105 + 106).

[5] Cf. Bedjan III, p. 412, *17–18* (Horn. "On 'the Kingdom of Heaven is Like unto Leaven,'" ET from Holy Transfiguration Monastery, in *The True Vine* 3 (1989), p. 47 (lines 41–42). Christ brought sweet fragrance to the world polluted by idolatry.

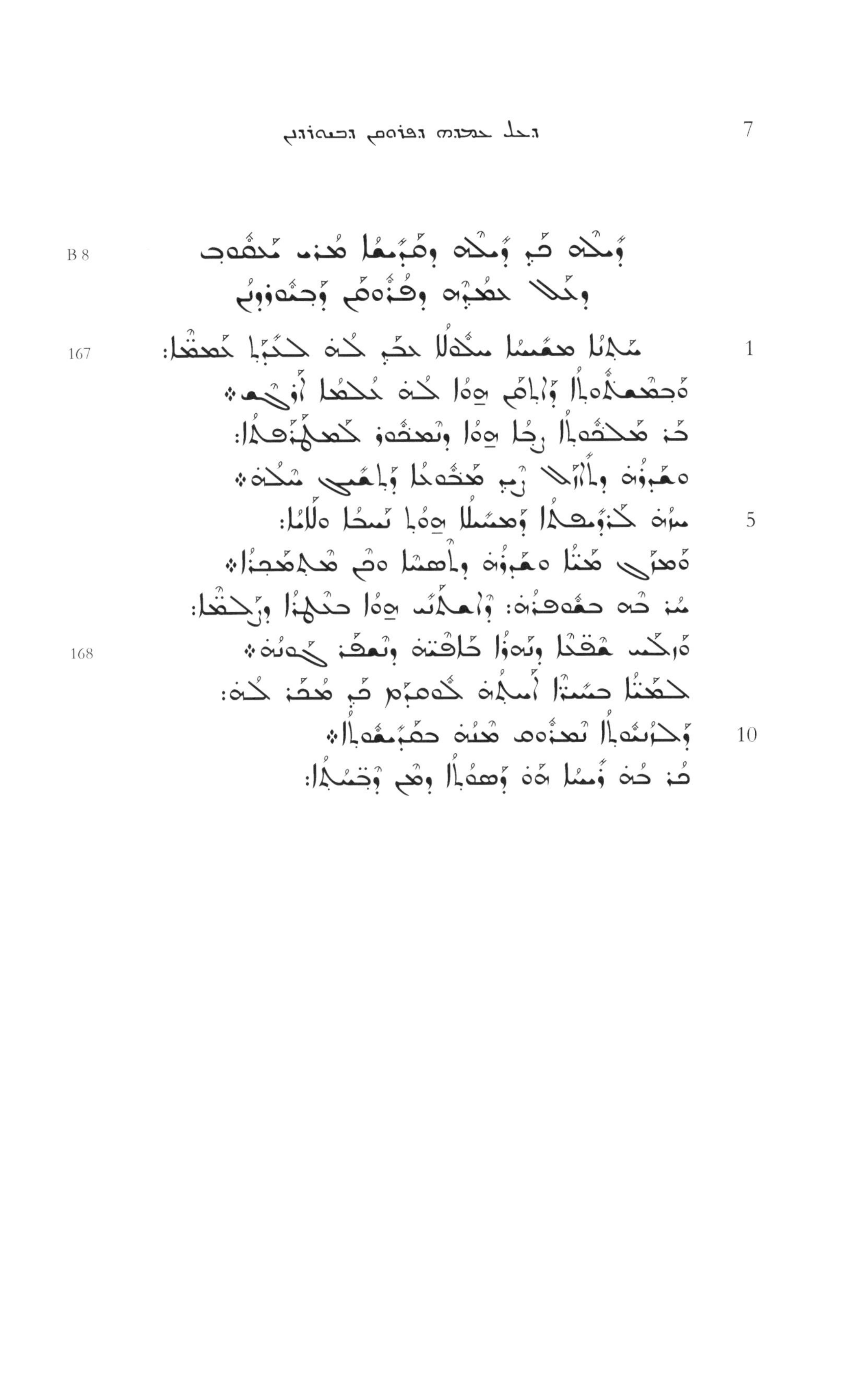

but He caused to pass unto her the wholesome waters to make her body fragrant.
She was made corrupt by the foulness of the oblations.
He besprinkled sanctity upon her so that she might be cleansed by it from defilement.[6]

15 In the womb of baptism[7] He placed the robe of glory[8]
and He sent the bride to go down to clothe herself from the waters.

JOHN THE BAPTIST, THE ADORNER OF THE BRIDE

He called His faithful servant, son of a barren woman, and sent him
beforehand to go and carry along the adornment to the bride before He comes.
John (the Baptist)[9] went out and carried the riches of the great treasure;

20 so that he might adorn the daughter of the poor as he was ordered.
He carried along and opened the trunk of the Spirit over the waters,
and brought out the garments to clothe the church in sanctity.

---

[6] Through baptism harlots are made virgins; cf. S. P. Brock, "Baptismal Themes," p. 337 (n. 67).

[7] Baptism is a 'second mother' in the sequence of Christ's stay in the womb of Mary and in the Jordan for the renewal of human nature. Hence, baptism is called 'an womb' that gives spiritual rebirth, cf. S. P. Brock, "Baptismal Themes," p. 334, (n. 46); T. Bou Mansour, *La Theologie de Jacques de Saroug*, I, pp. 253–254; cf. Narsai, *PO* 40, pp. 78/79 (lines 127–1128).

[8] 'Robe of glory': cf. Bedjan I, p. 197; III, p. 593; Alwan, *Création*, IV 455, 462; S. P. Brock, "Baptismal Themes," p. 336 (ns. 58,59,60); "Some Important Baptismal Themes," pp. 202–204; *Syriac Perspectives*, Ch. IV, pp. 98–104.

[9] John the Baptist is prefigured by Eliezer: cf. Gen 15:2; 24:2–4; cf. Homily "On the Betrothal of Rebecca," *OrSyr* 3 (1958), pp. 324–326 (esp. p. 324, n. 17).

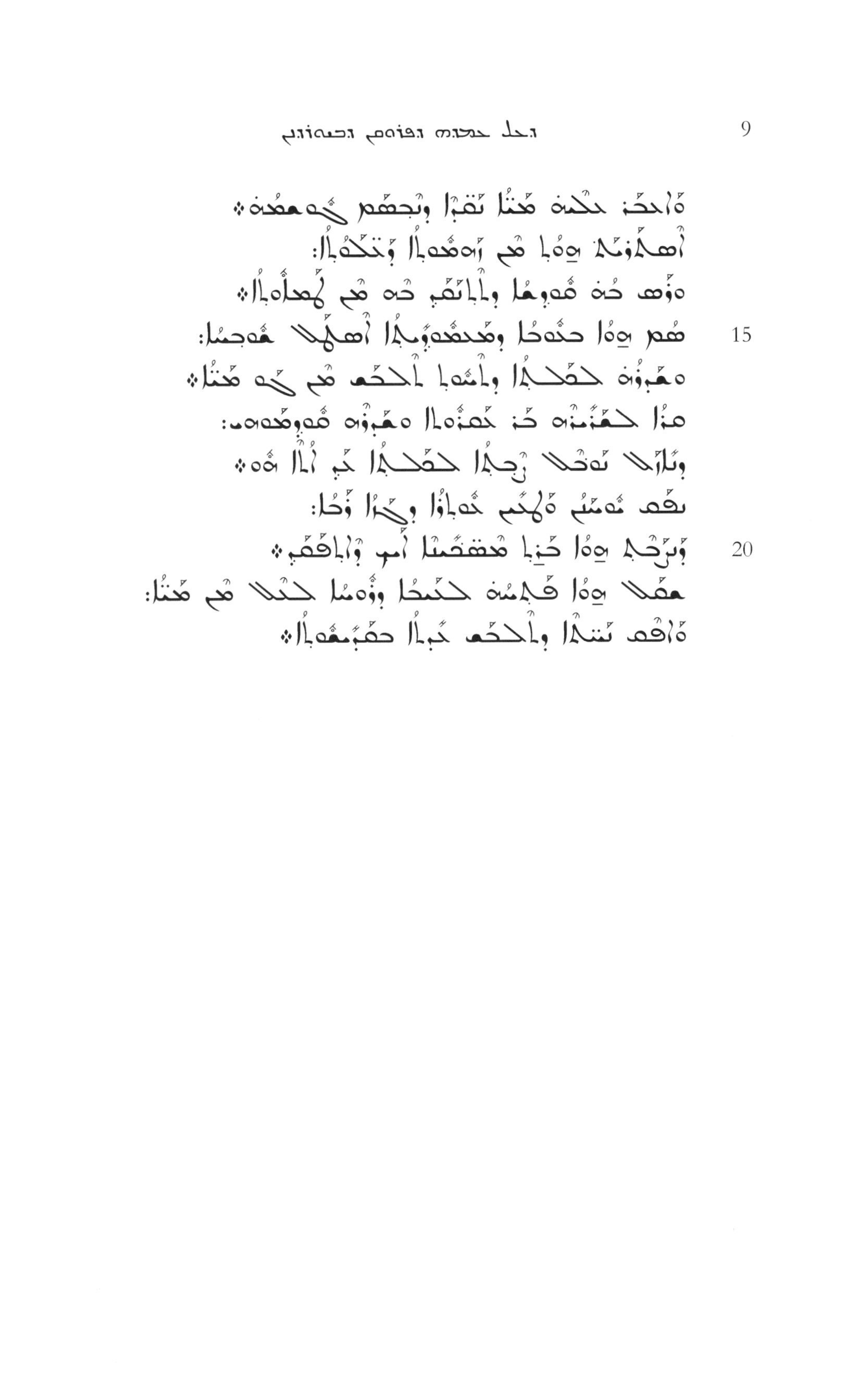

He showed her wonderful garments, that had not been seen by her,[10]
which had been made ready on the web of the divine abode.
25 The turbulent one captivated her through his intimate conversation bearing promises,
as he proclaimed the kingdom of heaven to the vagrants' daughter.
"Behold, the kingdom is close at hand, that is of heaven.   Matt 3:2
The Bridegroom himself has moved to come to you so that you might rejoice in Him."
He called the girl and she presented herself to be adorned
30 because she had learned that it was the royal Bridegroom who would be coming to her.

ISAIAH, THE INSTRUCTOR OF THE BRIDE

She invoked Isaiah to learn from him about John *[the Baptist]*,
"Who is this one who announces to me the kingdom on high?
Come, O Prophet, come, explain to me about the herald,
because I need to learn the truths from you.
35 I am accepting your word because it is for my sake;
For, behold, I have heard the speech of your discourse since a long time back.
You assured me about conversion in your prophecy.   Isa 1:27
Come, see, maybe the time has come that I may enter into it *[conversion]*.
See, what are the tidings of this one who proclaims serious matters,
40 while he himself appears in poverty.
His appearance is of renunciation but rich is the word of his proclamation.

---

[10] The robe woven in divine abode,' cf. Bedjan I, p. 211; S. P. Brock, "Baptismal Themes," p. 336, (n. 62). It is also 'a wedding garment': "Baptismal Themes," pp. 336–337 (ns. 64, 65, 66).

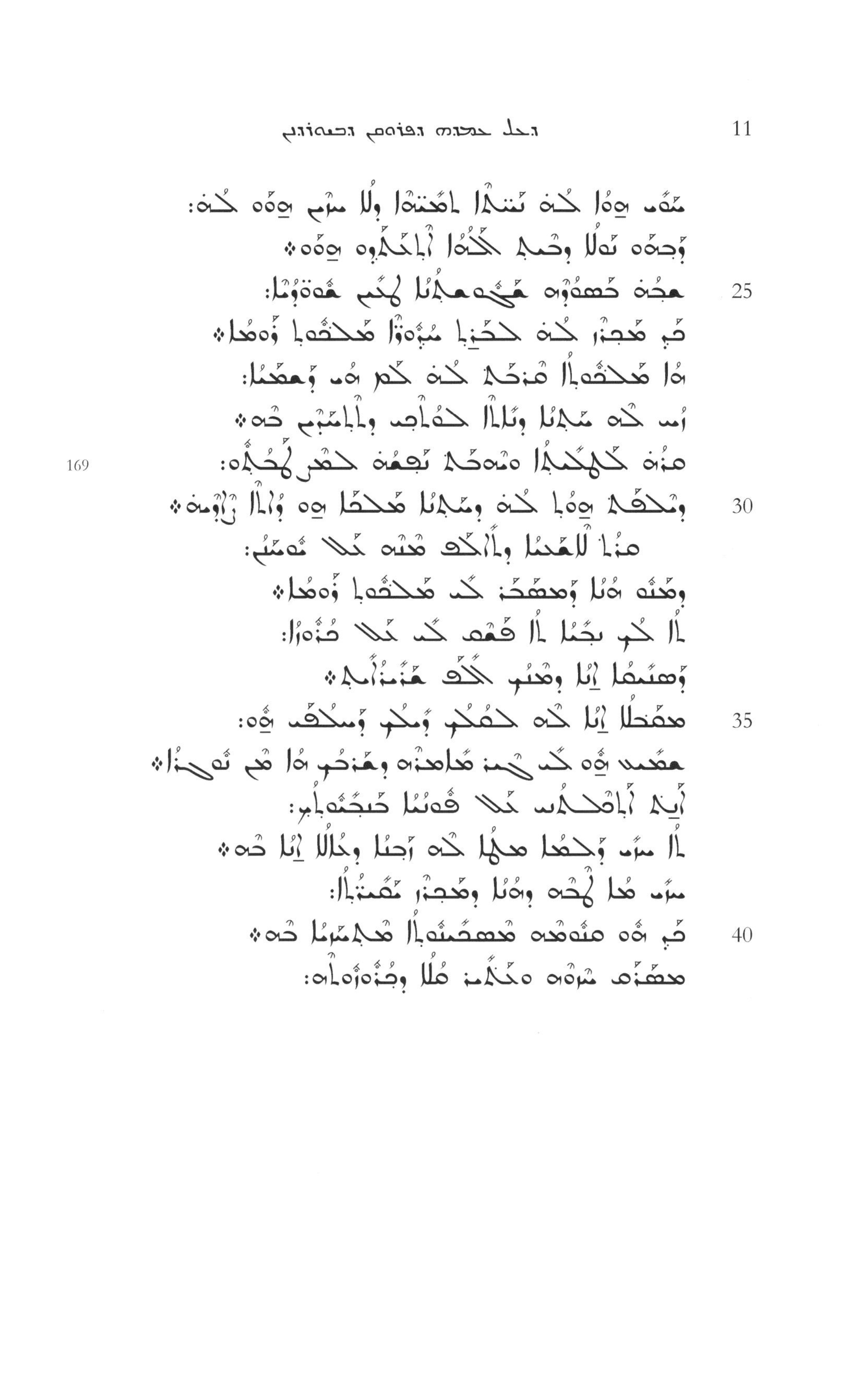

His attire is humble but his word is strong in the ears of all.
The man, when I saw him, was not speaking according to his stature
and the promise he sowed in my ears is not lowly as he is.

45 While he possessed utterly nothing, his word is magnificent.
He wanders in the desert and announces to me the kingdom on high.   Isa 40:3
Tell me, prophet, if he is genuine, I shall hear his words
and if he is not true let me not go astray through him as at other (times).
Your Lord is coming and I am preparing to enter before Him.

50 Reveal the truth to me, do not end up with accusation."
Isaiah approached to teach the Church about John the Baptist,
"Since he is a son of the mystery of the Bridegroom, your Lord, accept his words.
This is the voice that cries in the wilderness before the Son of the King;   Isa 40:3
Prepare, O you prepare, the way for the Lord in faith.

55 Go, descend, and be purified, do not excuse yourself from the herald.
He makes smooth the steep place so as to set in order the way for the King who is coming."

JOHN THE BAPTIST, THE TRUSTWORTHY OF THE BRIDE

The Church, the royal bride, approached towards John
and he began washing, cleansing, polishing and sanctifying her.
He became someone trustworthy to her since he laboured for her adornment as much as he could.

60 He taught and made her wise so that she might be corrected, for she was confused.
She heard his voice and gave heed after his words

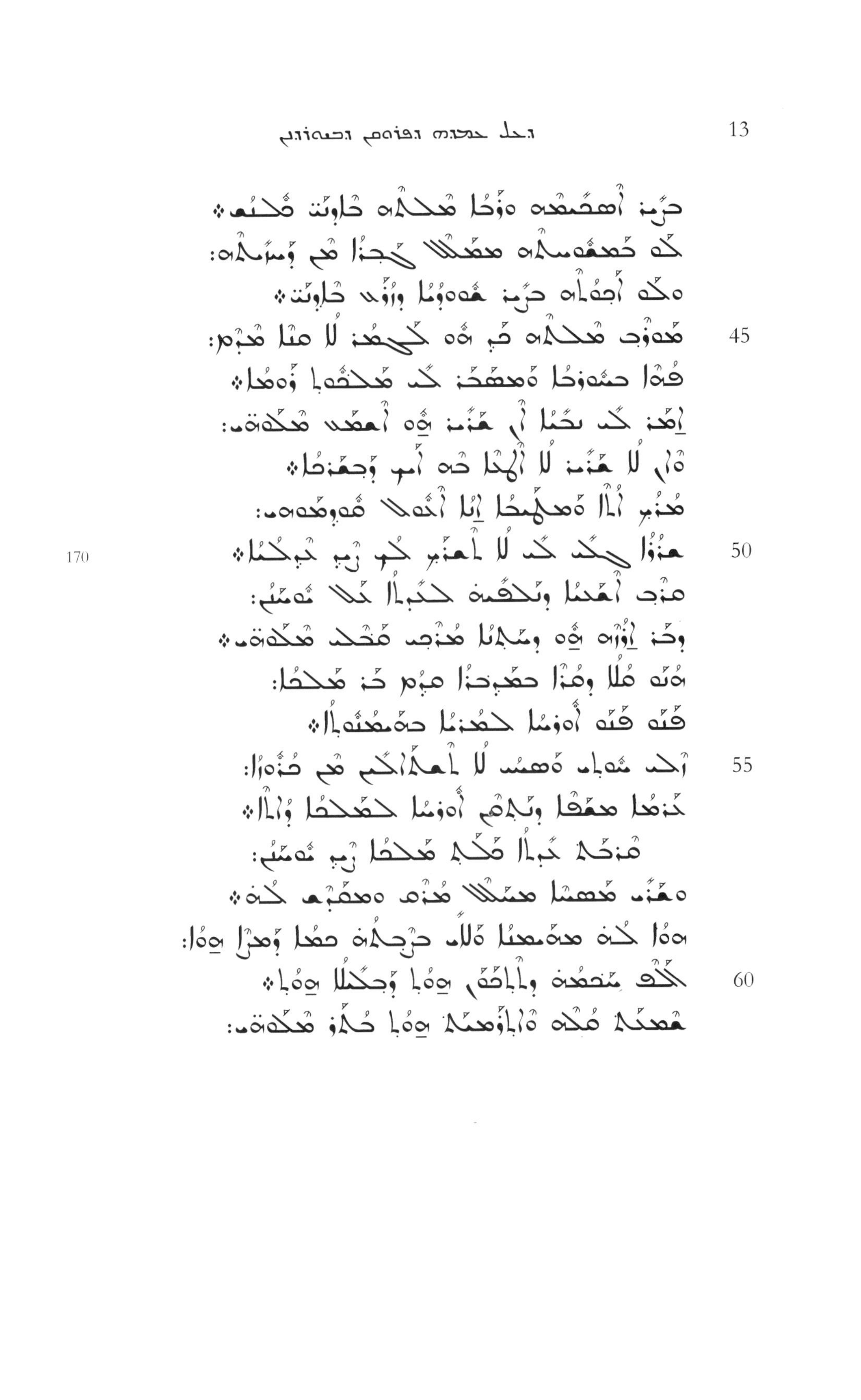

for she supposed that he was the Bridegroom to whom she was betrothed.[11]
She took hold of the servant affectionately, as though he were the Lord,
because the Messiah was concealed from her among the tribes.

65 The faithful servant saw that the betrothed bride clung to him,
and he began to shake all over and called out, "I am not the Bridegroom."
He thrust her away from him so that she might not be led astray by him because he was (only) a servant,
but he encouraged her to remain in the expectation of the Bridegroom while He was distant.
He humbled himself (saying), "I am not even worthy of His sandals," — Matt 3:11; Mark 1:7; Luke 3:16

70 as a faithful servant, in order to safeguard the presidency for his Lord.[12]
He noticed the young girl who set her eye upon him who was a Nazirite
and in haste he cut off the cause of scandal from her mind.
He bound her in an agreement to wait for the Bridegroom and not to look upon him,
proclaiming to her, "He comes after me but He is older than me." — Matt 3:11; Luke 3:16

THE TRUE BRIDEGROOM AWAITED BY THE CHURCH AND JOHN THE BAPTIST

75 She began gazing until she would perceive Him who was coming to her,
as she was examining the baptized one after another.
She herself was casting her eye for a moment upon many

---

[11] Ephrem also speaks of the true role of John the Baptist (lamp=John and Sun=Christ); cf. *HVirg* 5:9 [CSCO 223 (syri 94), p. 19].

[12] Cf. *HcHaer* 24:6.

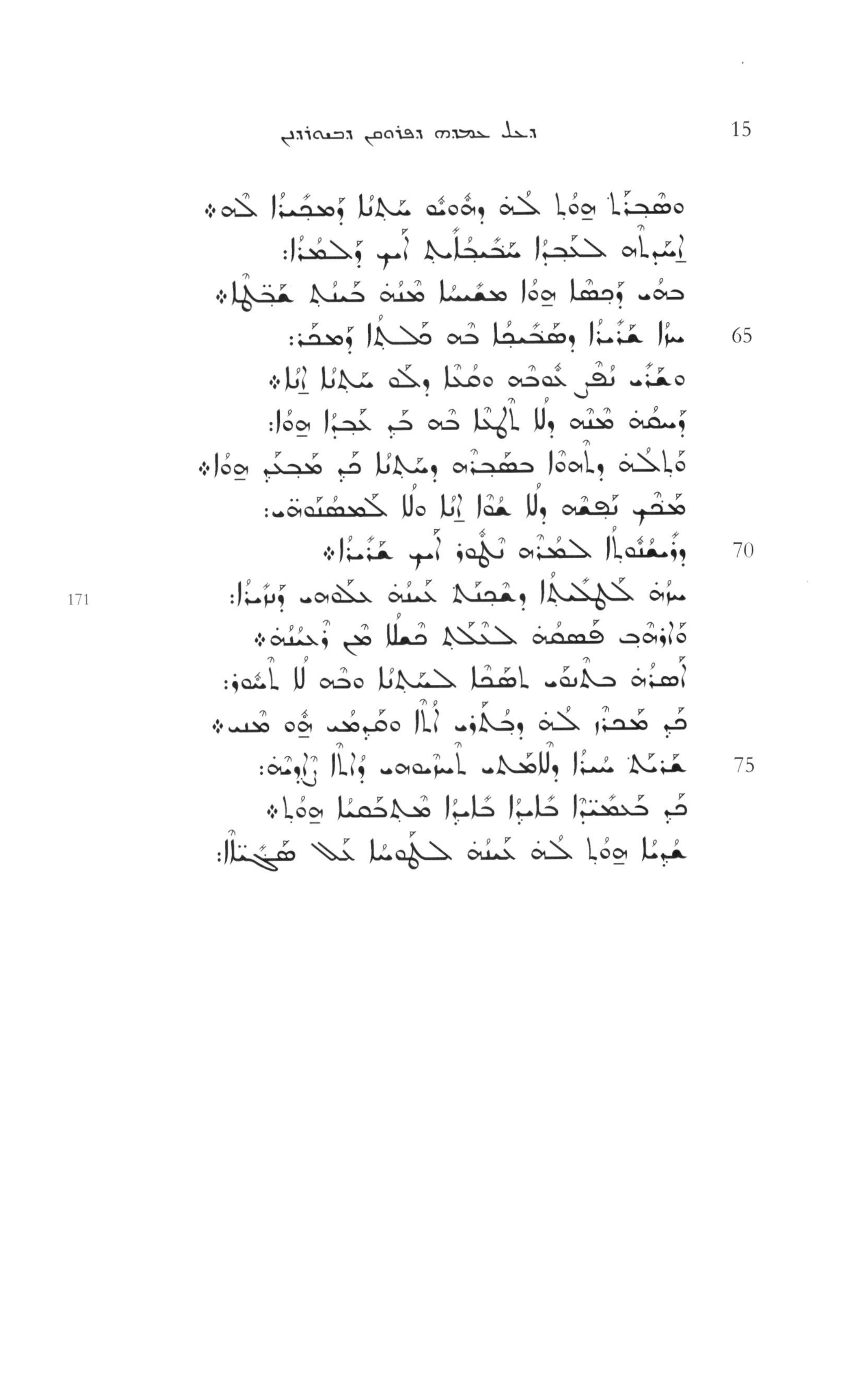

so that she might perceive among them the Only-Begotten to whom she is betrothed.
When someone was descending for baptism the crowds surrounded him
80 in order to take notice of him lest perchance he might be the Messiah who is coming.   Luke 3:15
The Church gathered herself and was present in the desert with John
fixing (her eyes) upon the wedding guests to see who is the Bridegroom.
She surrounded the river and cast her eyes along its rushing streams,
so as to receive the true Betrothed One from the waters.
85 The comely woman stood looking for the Bridegroom, when He would come,
in order to enter with Him into the womb of the waters to be sanctified.
Her arms extended, she waited for Him alongside the waters
so that when He bathed, He might be received in a holy manner.

JOHN THE BAPTIST'S EXPECTATION FOR THE MIGHTY VOICE OF THE FATHER

John too waited for Him as to when He would come
90 so that through Him his *[John's]* own baptism would be made perfect as it was imperfect.[13]
He was guarding the mystery that was between him and the Father,   John 1:33
and was looking for the Spirit who would bear witness concerning the True One.
When he was laying his hands to baptize those who were coming

---

[13] Jacob of Serugh explains the role of three baptisms; that of Old Testament washings (baptism of the law), the baptism of John the Baptist, and the baptism of Christ that fulfills all; cf. Bedjan I pp. 153–167 (a translation is in preparation by S. P. Brock)

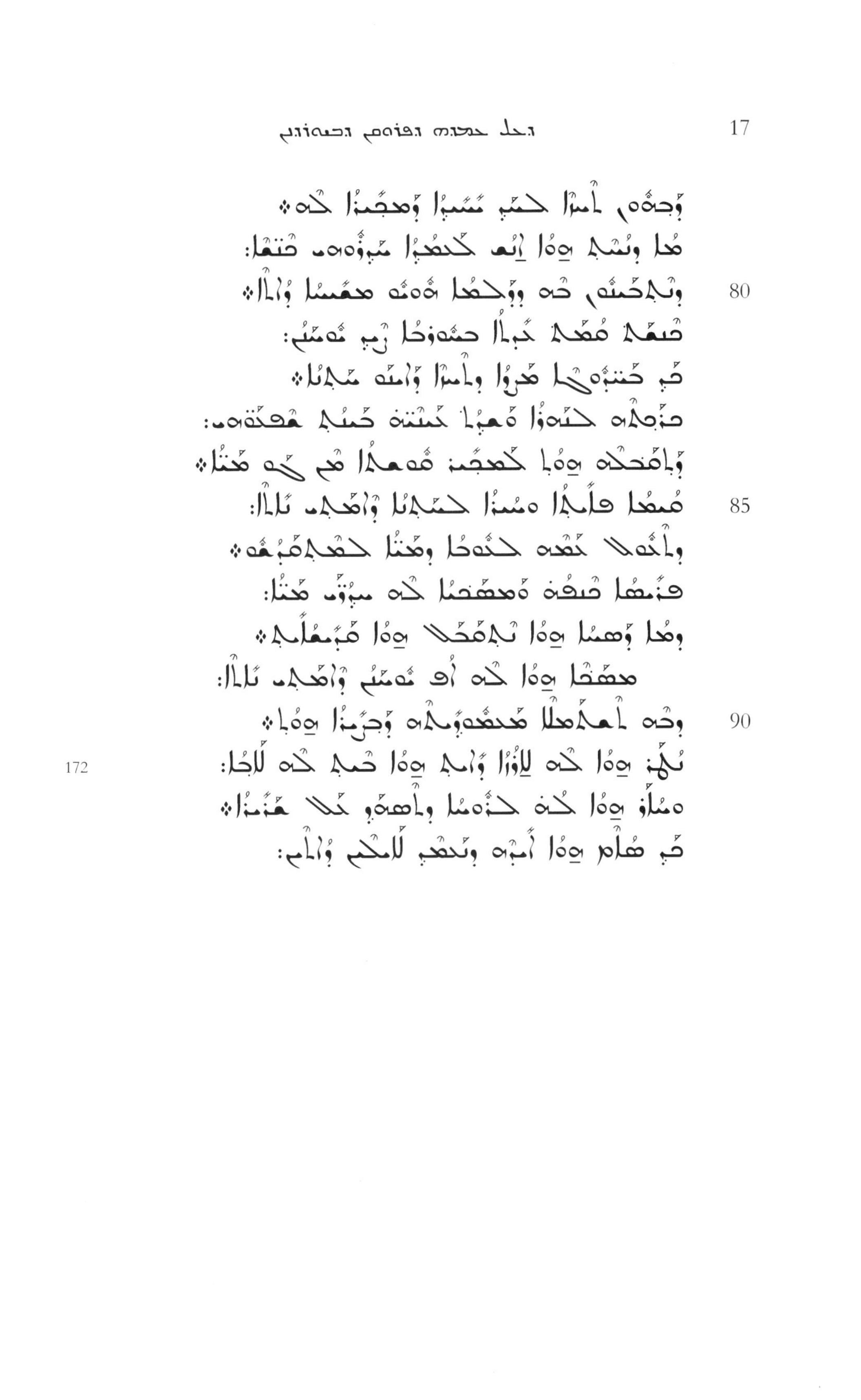

he used to gaze upward on account of the contract
that was there.
95 He made his eyes fly over many who were beside him
in order to perceive the One whom the Spirit, when
sent, would make manifest.
He was looking for that Bird, the mistress of heaven,
how it would descend and upon whom it would rest
so as to bear witness.
He was expecting the swift wings carrying the tips (of
the feathers)
100 to see who is the one whom they would be receiving
from the waters.
He thirsted to see the Bird that soars while not flap-   John 1:33,34
ping its wings,
for, when it would appear, it would be a witness concerning the redeemer.
He gave heed to the mighty voice of the Father   Matt 3:17;
to hear from it, the one concerning whom it was call-   Mark 1:11;
ing out, "He is my beloved Son."   Luke 3:22
105 The bride stood with the true servant, the son of a
barren woman
and she looked out for him until he would point out
that this is the Bridegroom.
She gives heed to him who shall declare to her regarding the Redeemer
whereas he waits for the Father to bear witness to His
Beloved One.
When someone came to descend to be baptized she
thronged around him,
110 (to see) whether he is the Bridegroom, so that she
might receive Him lovingly from him.
He said to the crowds, "Behold, among you stands   John 1:26
the Bridegroom,"
and this saying kindled fire in the bride.
He proclaimed again, "I am not worthy, not even of   Matt 3:11;
His sandals,"   Luke 3:16
and again he kindled her with the love as well as the
magnificence of Jesus.

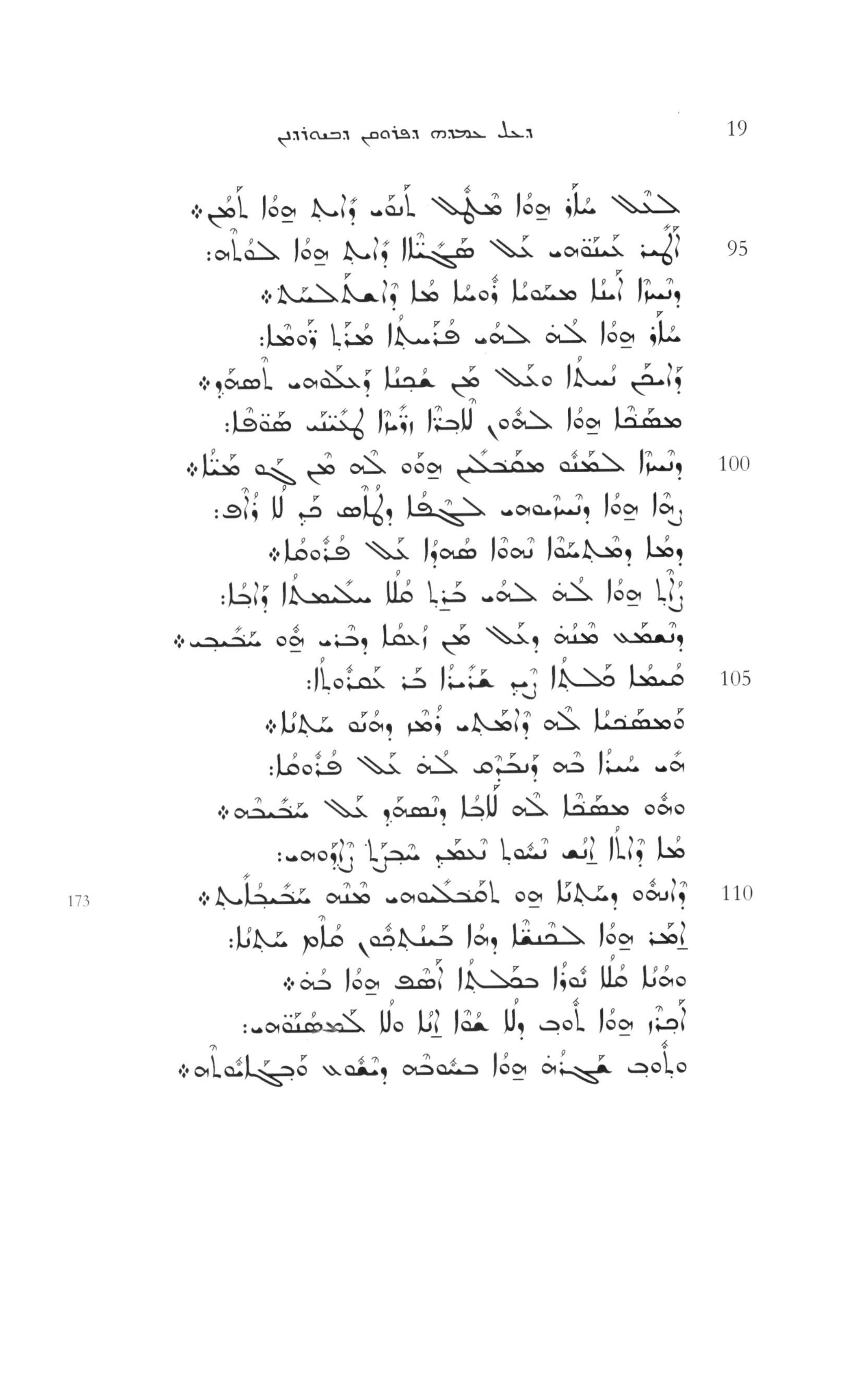

THE ORNATE BRIDE AND THE WEDDING-GUESTS EXPECTING 'THE WHITE GARMENT'

115 The 'bride of light' thrust herself forward and stood by the side of John
so that when he showed her who is the Bridegroom she might prostrate before Him.
The eye of the bride was cast upon everyone who was escorted to come
to be baptized until He came up (from the water).
Thousands were baptized but there was no Spirit descending[14] upon them.
120 Tens of thousands were bathed and the river was cool without the descent.
The crowds descended and the waters remained common[15] as they were (before).
Many came out (of the water) and the voice of the Father was hidden like Him.
And when the bride was made perfect with the ornaments of repentance,
and she was cleansed and came out from the waters of baptism,
125 And when the marriage feast was made ready with all its preparations,
yet the Bridegroom alone held Himself back from coming to visit His own.
When the washing took place for the wedding-guests and it *[the washing]* had cleansed them,
yet they were not clothed in the garments of the Spirit from the water.
And when all the peoples were standing stripped

---

[14] Cf. S. P. Brock, "Baptismal Themes," p. 341 (n. 92).

[15] Christ's baptism in Jordan made all baptismal waters gain the power of sanctification. Till then all Old Testamental ritual washings and that of John the Baptist remained imperfect or the waters remained as common waters without spiritual powers; cf. Bedjan I pp. 153–167 ("On the three Baptisms, of the Law, of John the Baptist and of Our Lord," a translation in preparation by S. P. Brock).

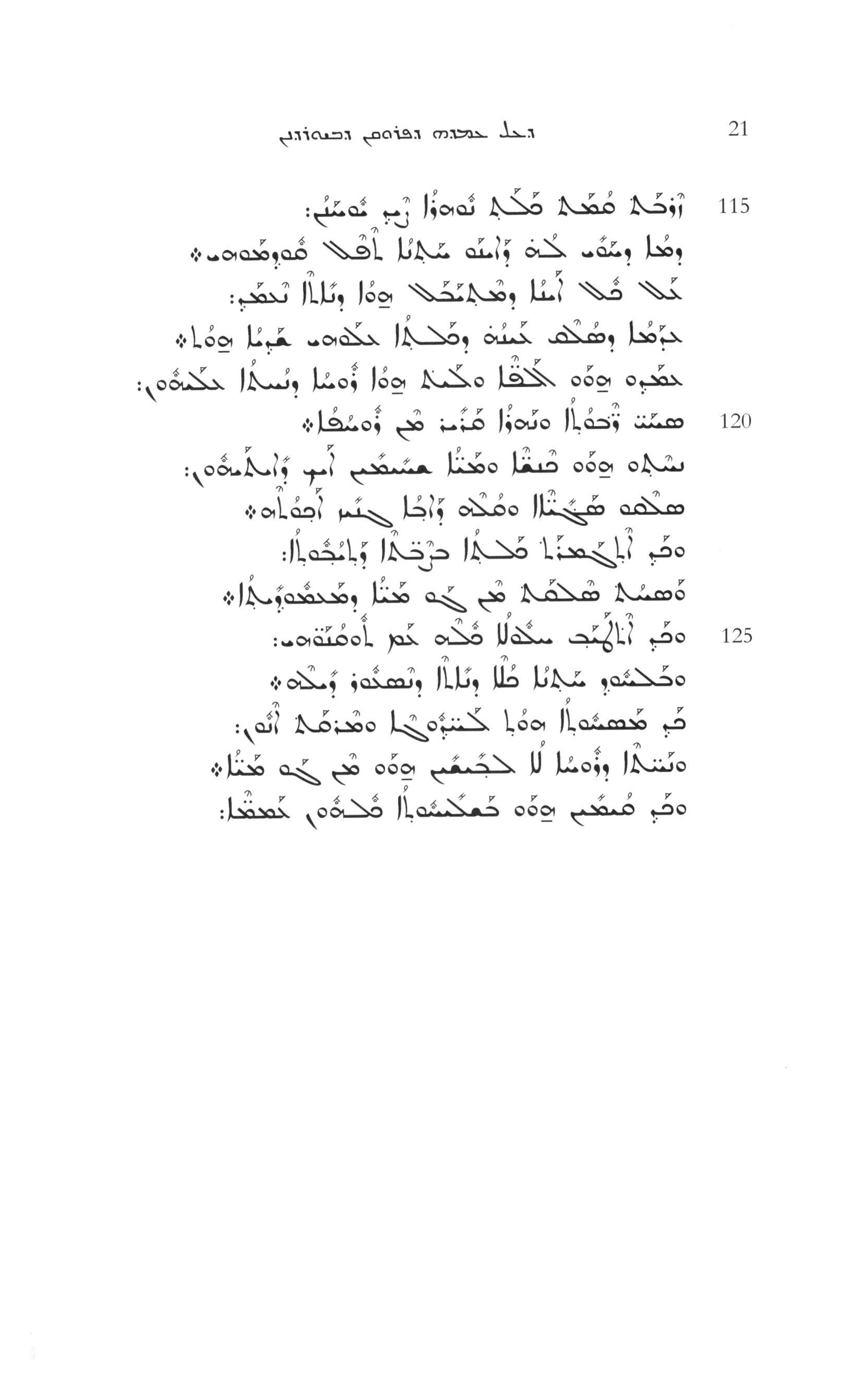

130   and were waiting for the Bridegroom to come and clothe them,
       and when the impurity of the bride was washed away in the water and she came up,
       and everyone looked for the white garments that the Bridegroom would bring,[16]
    and since baptism was deficient of forgiveness,
    and no one had received the Spirit of Holiness from the waters,

THE ARRIVAL OF THE BRIDEGROOM FOR BAPTISM

135   And when the entire wedding feast looked for the Bridegroom, where He might be,   *Luke 3:15*
    (then) the Royal Son came out from among the crowds to come to the river.
    And when He was far off, the baptismal water became fervent in response to Him,
    and the river overflowed and silently proclaimed Him.
    The Holy Spirit came out by itself and stood above the water
140   and the heat of His power kindled them *[the waters]*,
    His fire kindled among the rushing streams before He descended
    and the river exulted with the great fervent heat of the Flame.
    The baptismal water earnestly desired Him who had come to it
    like that horn of anointing in response to David.   *1 Sam 16:1–13*
145   It was not that it became fervently heated at His arrival so as to render Him holy, for He is (already) holy;

---

[16] 'white garments' cf. S. P. Brock, "Baptismal Themes," p. 336 (n. 63).

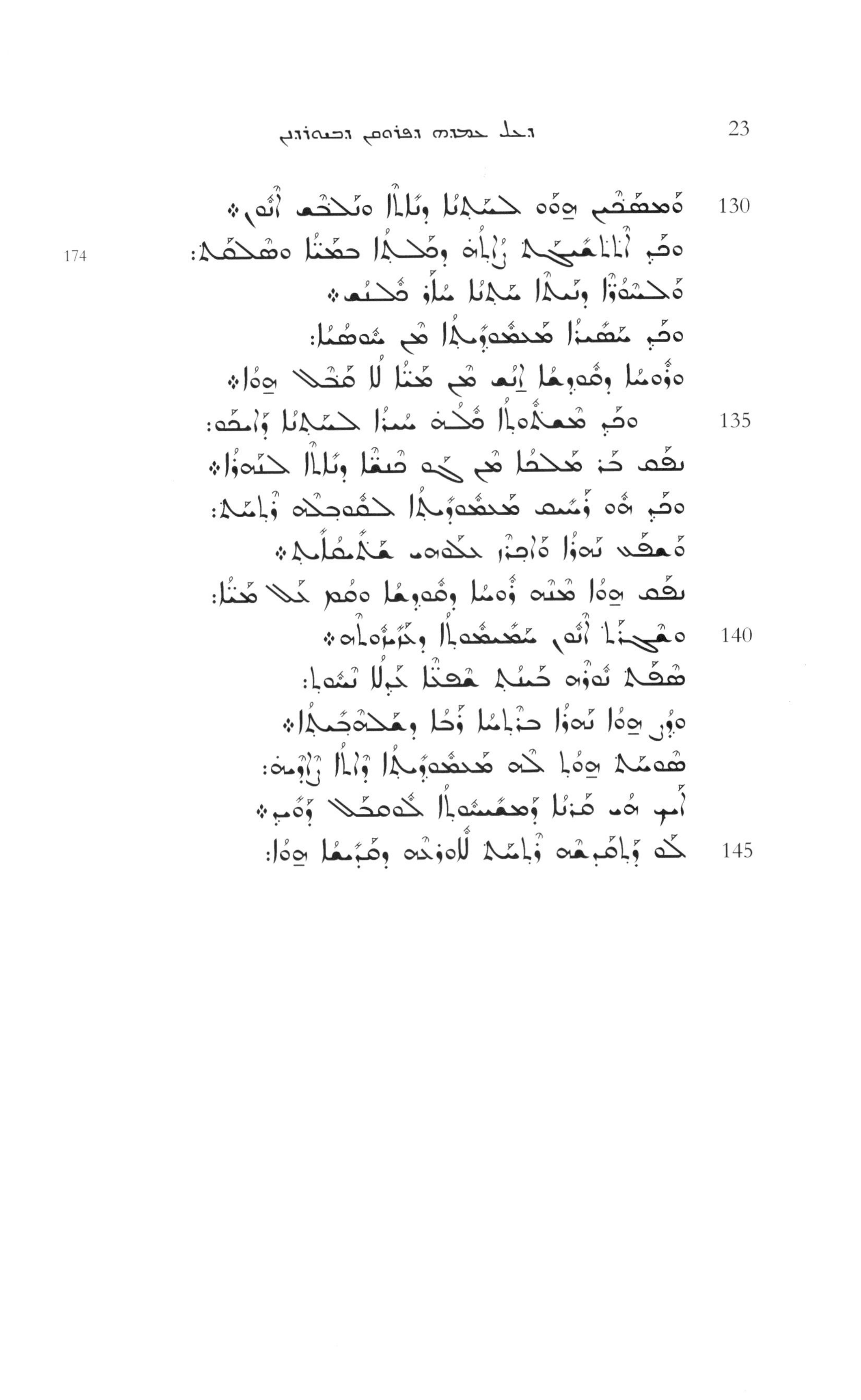

It embraced Him so that its womb[17] might be sanctified by Him.
It exulted in Him because He was its accomplishment and consummation
and it stretched out its arm so that the holiness of the Son might be received into it.
John noticed the river which grew hot, and its abounding streams were transformed
150 and he himself understood that that Holy One had come to baptism.
He drew back his hand so as not to baptize those who were coming,
so that Christ, the Bridegroom, might be held back and stand alone.
He shouted among the crowds and drove them away from the riverside
so that all might know that for whose sake baptismal waters grew hot.
155 He pushed back the flock to drive itself away from the fountain,
in order to separate the Sacrificial Lamb that it might go out from the flock.   Lev 16:20–31
He made signs to the wedding-guests and they offered Him place among the crowds
in order that the Bridegroom might appear in glory to all the peoples.
The crowds that encircled the baptismal waters fled
160 and the Son of the Kingdom stood alone as a solitary.

THE BRIDE INSTRUCTED BY JOHN THE BAPTIST AND DAVID

The trustworthy servant made haste to announce about the Redeemer to the free-born woman.

---

[17] For other texts of Jacob of Serugh on 'baptismal womb,' see S. P. Brock, "Baptismal Themes," p. 334 (n 46); "Some Important Baptismal Themes," p. 197; Ephrem *HFid* 10:17; Narsai's Homily 22 (see A. Mingana, *Homiliae et Carmina* I, p. 364; ET by R. H. Connolly, *Liturgical Homilies of Narsai*, p. 41); PO 40, pp. 78/79 (lines 127–128).

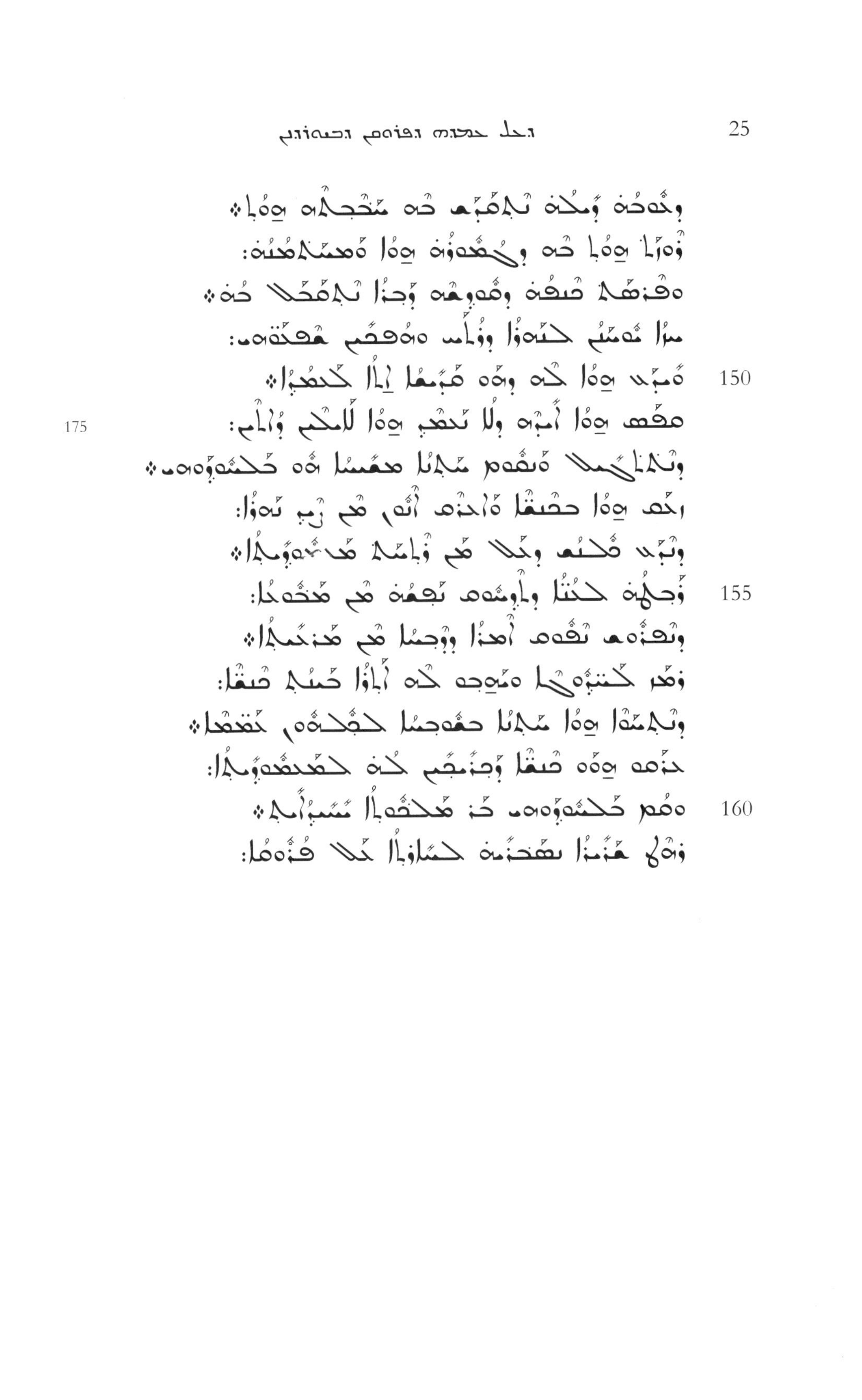

He summoned the chaste woman to show her who her Lord is.
"O Church, from the beginning, I betrothed you to this Bridegroom;
in the hope of this One I have held you from the time I came.
165 This is the Lamb who presented Himself to become a sacrifice.
This One carries away the sin of the world in His being sacrificed.   John 1:29
Behold, for a long time I had assured you about this One.
In the name of this One I have been keeping you waiting for Him.
For this One I guarded you with watchful care like a faithful servant.
170 Thank Him on account of me for I had not left you behind to be captivated by me."
And when the royal bride became instructed by John,
behold, David, the singer of the Spirit, approached singing to her:
"Hear, my daughter and look and give heed to the glorious things.   Ps 45:10
Forget your people and those of your father's house because they are wavering.
175 Yes, in truth He is your Lord; approach and adore Him;
Do not be wavering about the Redeemer who has come to you."
The Church learned from John as well as from David
and she became assured that He is the Bridegroom to whom she is betrothed.
She came near and stood there to see how He too is being baptized
180 so that when He ascended from the waters she might fall down before Him.

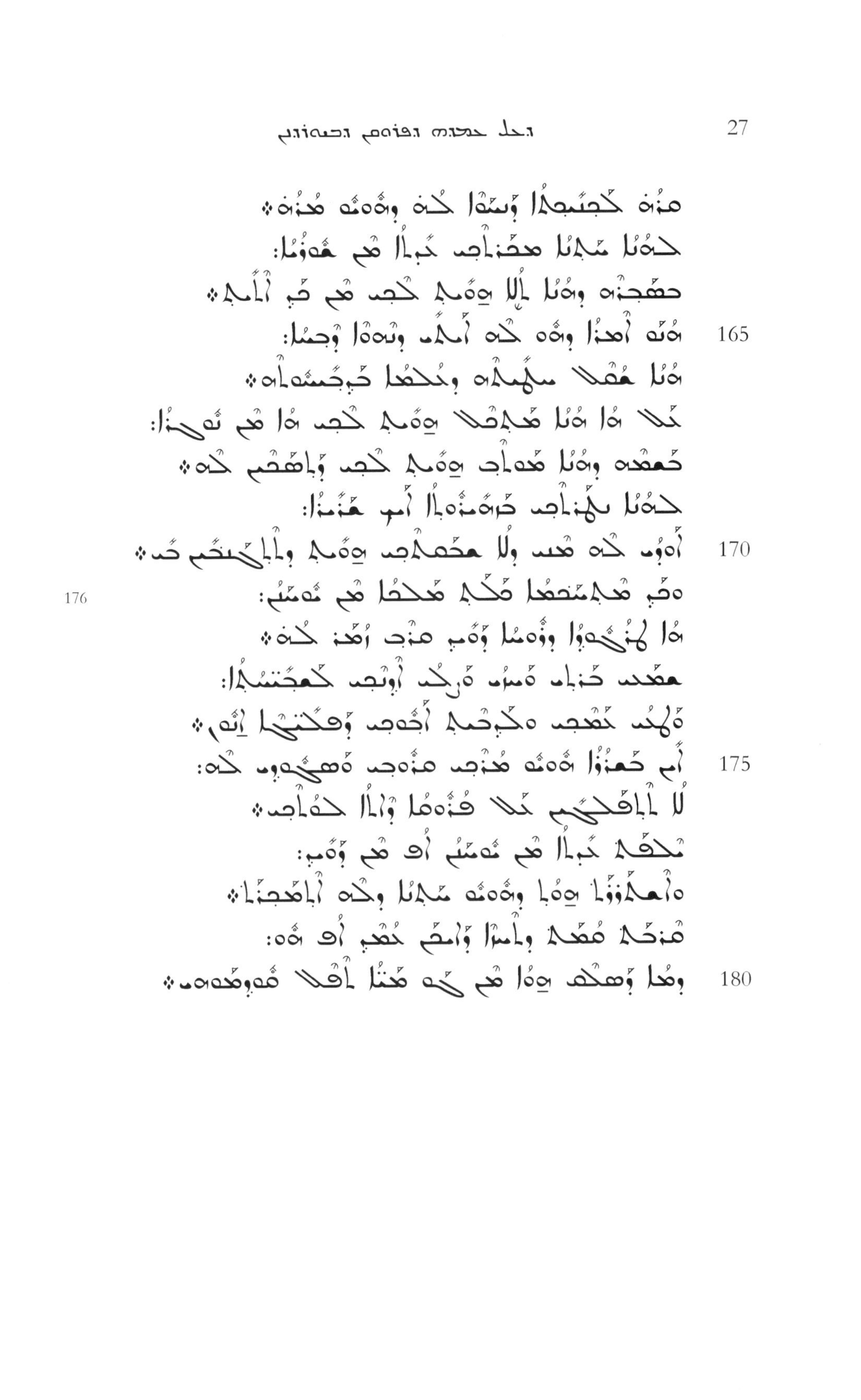

176

JOHN'S REFUSAL TO BAPTIZE CHRIST[18]

Christ approached John to be baptized by Him
John perceived Him and withdrew his hand from the Fiery One.
He bowed his head before the Son while saying to Him,
"It is I who ought to be baptized by you because you are the Holy One.   Matt 3:14

185   I was expecting you that I might commit baptism to you.[19]
Behold, your treasure is for you and therefore allow me henceforth to take a little rest.
I looked after the office, but governorship is not mine.
Remain in your rank: I do not have authority over your power.
A king does not receive authority from a pauper;

190   It is from the crown the ranks of all powers proceed.
What is there in baptism that is not yours?
and what is lacking in you so that you should descend to take (anything) from the water?
If it is pardon,[20] it proceeds from you for mankind; and if it is forgiveness,
the forgiveness of debts too is yours.

195   If it is priesthood, the whole of it is in you because you are the High Priest;
and if it is kingship, you are the one who fastens the crowns for the kings.[21]
Holiness proceeds from you to mankind:
and if it is priesthood, behold the world exists by your right hand.

---

[18] It is important to note the close affinity between the following texts, the present passage, lines 181–326, and the other of Ephrem (*HEpiph* 14:7–47), even textual similarity can be noticed. See also Narsai, *PO* 40, pp. 84–86 (lines 229–276).

[19] Cf. Ephrem's Prose Homily 'On Our Lord' (see *SdDN* 53, 54).

[20] Or 'propitiation.'

[21] Cf. *HAzym* 5:14.

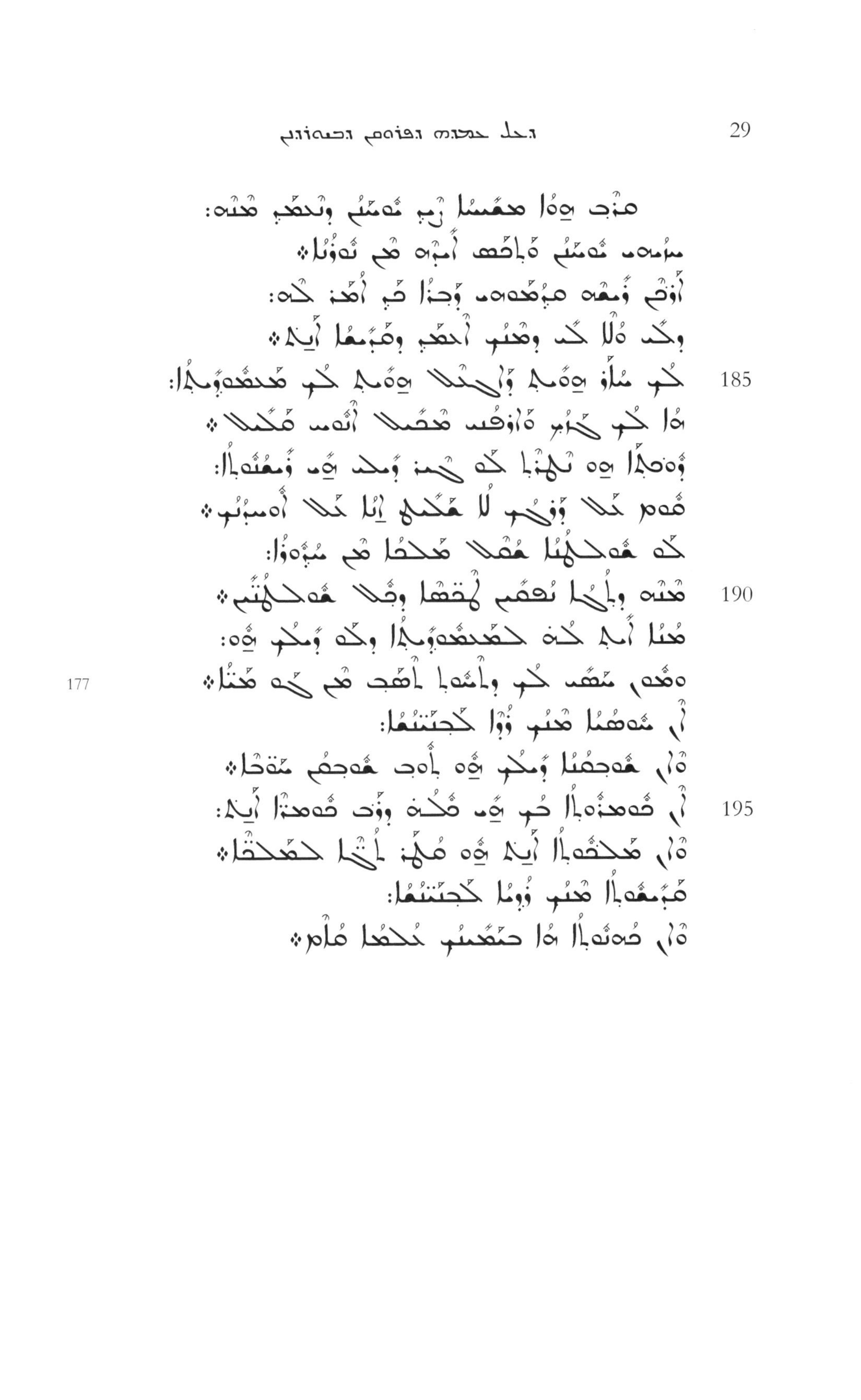

	And seeing that the fullness of divinity is with you,	Col 2:9
200	what is there for the small river to accomplish in you?"	

CHRIST'S DEMAND FOR BAPTISM FOR THE RECOVERY OF ADAM

	Our Lord says: "I am not lacking but in one thing:	
	the recovery of Adam who was lost from me is being sought by me.	
	Allow me to descend to seek Adam, the fair image,	Gen 1:26
	and when I shall find him the whole of my desire shall be fulfilled.	
205	It became a great search for me in his case and on account of that I have come,	
	and it would be a deficiency if I cannot find the lost one.	
	The recovery of him, that alone is what is lacking with me:	
	To regain Adam who was willing to perish at the hands of the evil one.[22]	
	In this recovery my desire will come to perfection,	
210	because Adam is needed by me to enter into his inheritance.	
	Therefore, allow me to descend to cleanse the image that has become faded,	
	lest it too would remain deficient, should you withhold me.	
	That loving kindness which summoned me to come to birth,	Titus 3:4
	that has again called me to come to baptism too.	
215	The great mercy has drawn me to descend to become a new born babe.	
	It is that (mercy) which drew me to descend to become baptized.[23]	

---

[22] Cf. *CNis* 36:2, in a different context Ephrem alludes to Christ's seeking Adam who was imprisoned in Sheol.

[23] Cf. *HEpiph* 10:3, 9; Ephrem goes even further and says that Christ led all to the bridal chamber as the goal of his journey.

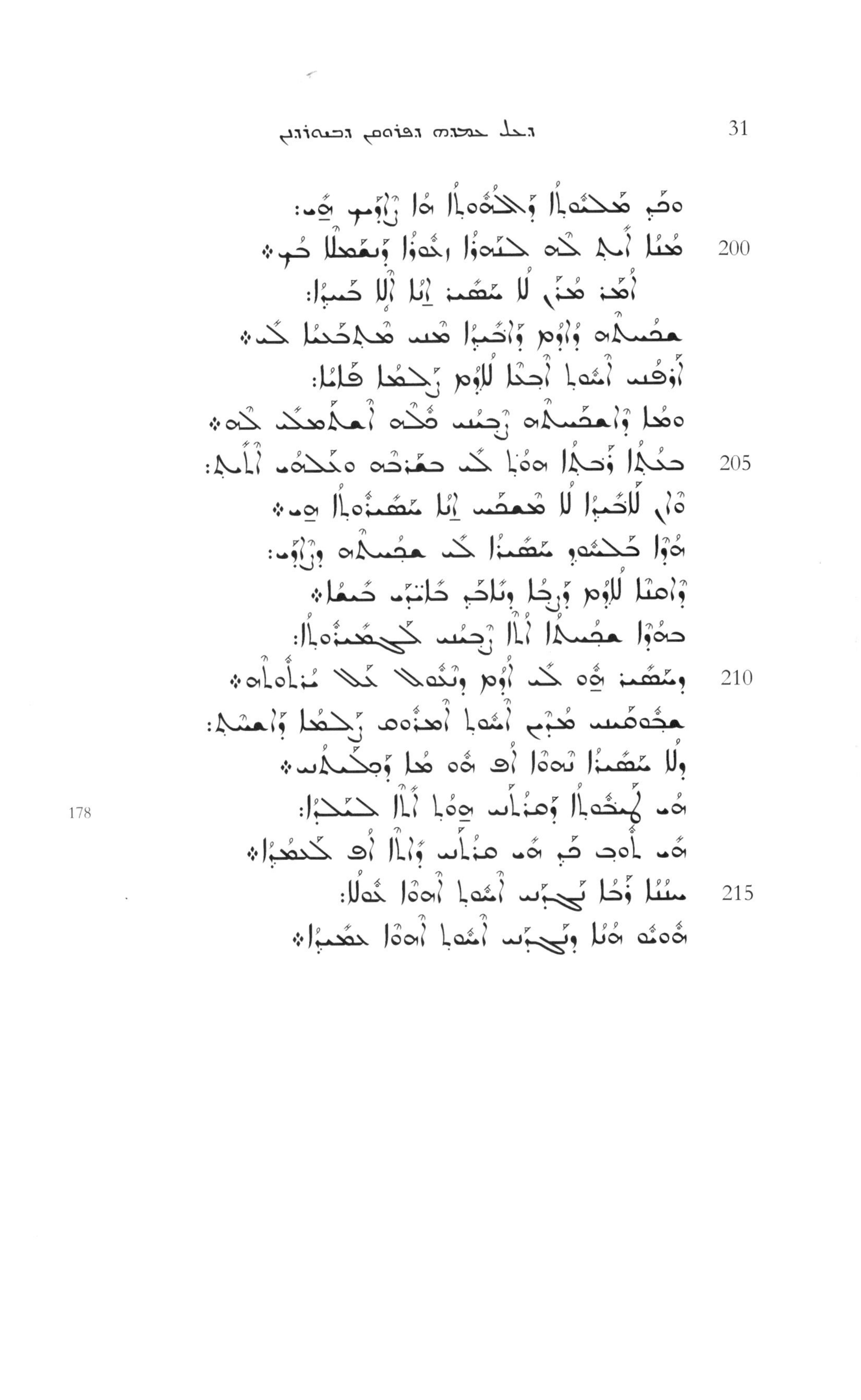

The baptismal womb is not narrower than the belly,
and the water of the river is not more dark than the womb.
If you imagine that you are rendering honour to me,
220   it would have been right for you to withhold me also from conception and nativity.
If it is a dishonour to me, which place is meaner,
the womb of flesh or the dignity of baptism?
If you had withheld me from coming to conception while you were within your mother,
it would have been easy for you to hold back so that I would not also be baptized, as I was sent.
225   If you had turned me away from that state of being born,
come, turn me away from the order of baptism.
If you had removed me from the swaddling-clothes and I had not been wrapped round,
drive away from me the waves of the river so that they do not cover me.
If you had blocked me from sucking the mean milk,
230   you would have withheld me from the fountain lest I descend to it.
If you had withheld me from dwelling in the womb of Mary
I would also have passed over myself from the womb of baptism.
And now I have travelled and come into this road of those born,
unless I have perfected it, how is it possible that I should turn away from it?
235   Therefore it is becoming for me too, in accordance as I was sent,
that the entire way upon which I have come down should be fulfilled in me."

John's Confession of His Inability before the Royal Son

John shrank back trembled, terrified by the Royal Son.
He adored Him and confessed, as he passionately made supplication:
"Lord, I pray, I am not fit to approach you.

ܕܥܠ ܚܟܡܬܗ ܕܦܘܠܘܣ ܘܕܚܘܒܗ

ܠܐ ܢܟܣܪ ܚܘܒܗ ܘܡܚܣܕܘܬܐ ܠܚܕ ܡܢ ܕܪܓܗ܀
ܘܡܟܢܐ ܘܢܗܘܐ ܠܚܕ ܡܢ ܡܕܡܚܐ ܠܐ ܫܦܘܕܝܢ܀
ܐܢ ܐܝܟܢܐ ܦܫܝܩ ܐܝܕܐ ܟܕ ܡܫܐܠܐܢܐ ܠܟ܆
ܙܘܥ ܗܘܐ ܠܟ ܘܐܢ ܡܢ ܟܠܗܘܢ ܡܟܐ ܐܓܠܣܬ܀   220
ܐܢ ܪܓܙܐ ܗܘ ܟܕ ܐܒܐ ܘܐܕܝܐ ܥܡܠܐ ܗܘܝܬ܆
ܕܪܗܐ ܘܚܣܕܐ ܐܘ ܪܚܡܐ ܘܡܚܣܕܘܬܐ܀
ܐܠܐ ܡܟܚܕܝܣ ܘܐܢܐ ܚܟܝܡܐ ܒܝ ܐܝܕܐ ܚܠܝܡܝܢ܆
ܩܒܠ ܗܘܐ ܘܠܐܦܬܘܗܝ ܘܐܡܠܐ ܐܚܕܝ ܐܡܪ ܘܐܥܒܕܚܬܡ܀
ܐܢ ܐܘܩܕܠܝܣ ܡܢ ܗܘ ܘܥܘܓܠܐ ܘܡܟܒܝܪܬܐ܆   225
ܐܠܐ ܐܘܩܕܣ ܗܢܘ ܘܐܓܚܗܐ ܘܡܚܣܕܘܬܐ܀
ܐܢ ܐܚܣܝܐܢܣ ܡܢ ܙܕܘܘܬܐ ܘܠܐ ܕܪܟܐ ܗܘܐܠܝ܆
ܠܗܢܘ ܡܢ ܙܐܘܥ ܢܓܠܐ ܘܢܗܘܐ ܘܠܐ ܒܟܣܘܕܝܣ܀
ܐܢ ܟܠܝܗܣܝܣ ܘܠܐ ܐܣܠܕܘܗܝ ܗܘܘܐܠܝ ܡܠܟܐ ܥܡܝܐ܆
ܛܠܐ ܗܘܐܠܝ ܟܕ ܡܢ ܡܟܚܘܕܢܐ ܘܠܐ ܐܫܘܝ ܠܕܗ܀   230
ܐܠܐ ܡܟܚܕܝܣ ܘܠܐ ܐܥܙܐ ܗܘܘܐܠܝ ܕܚܣܝܩܗ ܘܡܕܝܢܬܡ܆
ܠܟܕ ܗܘܘܐܠܝ ܟܕ ܐܘ ܡܢ ܚܘܒܗ ܘܡܚܣܕܘܬܐ܀
ܘܗܘܡܗܐ ܘܙܘܥܒܝܕ ܘܐܠܐܠܝܕ ܟܐܘܢܬܐ ܗܘ ܘܡܟܬܒܐ܆
ܐܠܐ ܚܝܣܕܢܐܘܗ ܐܢܛ ܥܪܝܢܐ ܘܐܘܩܥܡܝ ܗܢܘܗ܀
ܐܘ ܗܘܡܢܐ ܐܠܐ ܟܕ ܚܡܢ ܐܡܪ ܘܐܥܒܕܚܬܡ܆   235
ܘܒܐܡܠܐ ܚܕ ܦܠܟܗ ܐܘܪܝܫܐ ܘܚܠܡܗ ܝܣܠܝܐ܀
ܚܕܪ ܫܡܥܢܝ ܐܪܗ ܕܐܣܠܐܘܘ ܡܢ ܟܕ ܡܟܚܟܐ܆
ܗܝܝ ܠܗ ܟܐܘܒܕ ܒܝ ܡܟܪܟܣܘܕ ܘܕܗܘܡܥܠܝܕ܀
ܚܕܐ ܐܢܐ ܡܪܝ ܠܐ ܗܥܩܡ ܐܢܐ ܘܐܠܐܣܪܬ ܠܟ܆

240	The husk is too feeble to set its hand upon the Flame.
	How can a straw lay hold of the Flame?
	Or a dry stick set its hand upon the Coal of Fire?
	The fervent heat of your energy has kindled itself in the river and behold, it has set it on fire
	and how is it that you will not burn up the hands of flesh?
245	Nor is there any necessity that you be baptized by me, as though you were lacking,
	so that there should not be division in the world, (on the grounds) that you are deficient.
	Go, Royal Son, redeem the captives, for behold, they are looking for you.
	You need to take no armour for yourself from the water.
	Your crown is eternal and is not changed;
250	From the treasury of baptism you are not going to be filled.
	Press on with your journey: Behold, the captives thirst to see you;
	you are not looking for the company of anyone to go with you.
	You are born upon the purple of the Father from His essence;
	and you do not need to be clothed from this place and thus to redeem.
255	It is the right time on the earth, do not delay from the redemption.
	Proceed forth, go on to snatch the captivity of the peoples from the persecutors.
	O King of kings, the kingdom of the Father and yours is the same;
	as regards power, you will not become stronger from here.

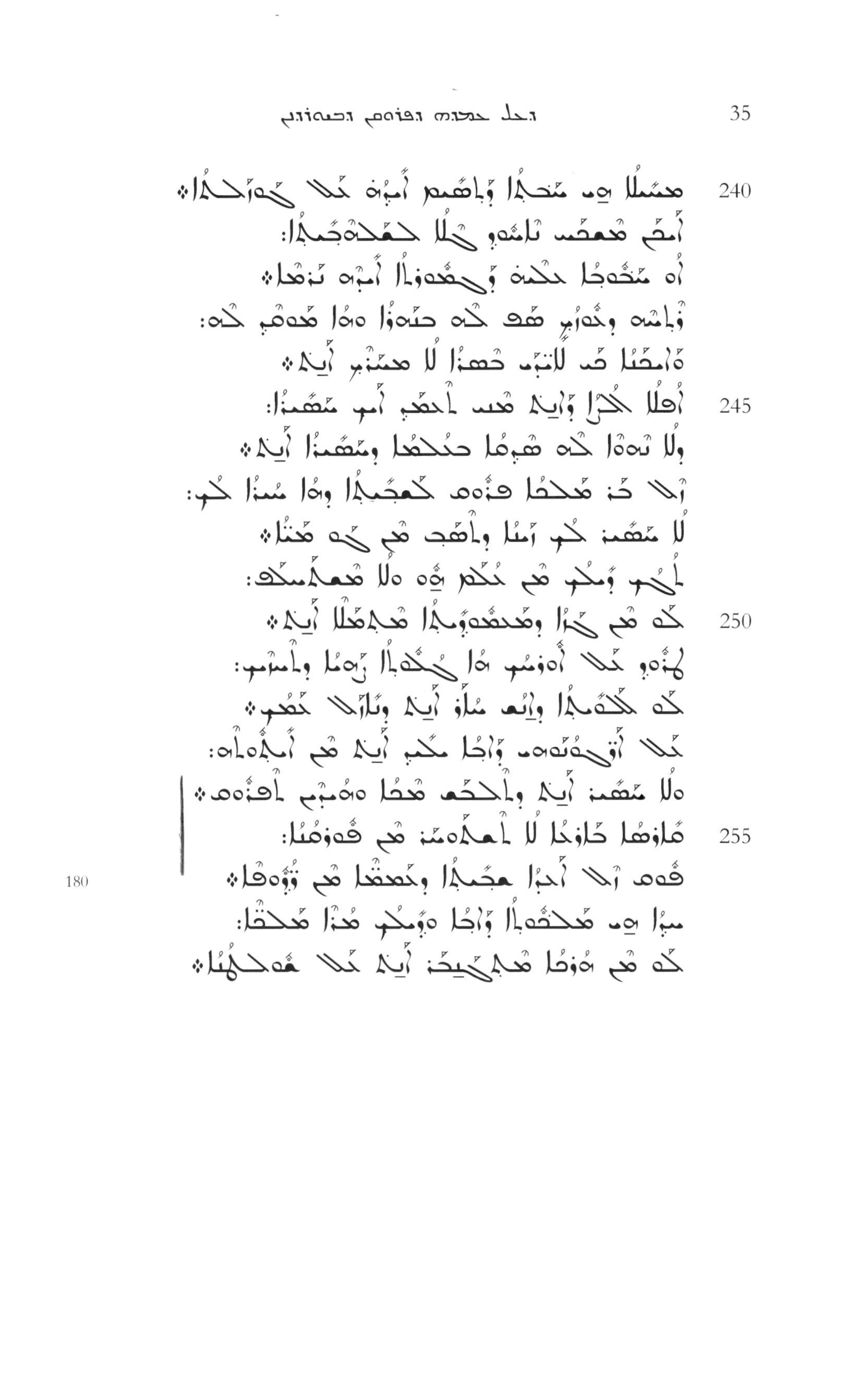

180

Behold, the captivity passed beyond the inhabited land;[24] Why are you waiting?

260 Go forward, turn back the captivity from the stumbling blocks through which it has gone out.

Behold, the captors have plundered the region, hasten your course (of action);

proceed forth, go, and make the captivity return because it had gone out of your dominion.

There is no addition in baptism with regard to yourself,

and for what (purpose) then are you endeavouring to descend and wash?"

THE REASON AND RIGHTEOUSNESS OF CHRIST'S DESCENT FOR BAPTISM

265 "Be silent, John, you are not making any addition upon me,

waters are in need of sanctification which will be provided by me.

I descended to the fountain not to take up a shield for myself

but to forge mighty armour for warriors.[25]

I am anxious to cleanse humanity[26] in the contest of battle

270 so that every one who comes to fight should fight like me.

I am instituting baptism as an armoury;

Unless man has entered and clothed himself[27] from it, he will not fight.

---

[24] Cf. Bedjan I, pp. 278, *9–18*; 280, *11–16*; 281, *3* – 282, 5 (Homily 'On the Prodigal Son'). Going into captivity is interpreted as alienation from God and setting oneself as slave and captive under evil one in a desert land.

[25] Baptism as the armour from the water and fire: cf. Bedjan II, pp. 677, *11–12*; 679, *3–4*; 687, *11–12*; S. P. Brock, "Baptismal Themes," p. 337 (n. 68); see also Ephrem *HEpiph* 5:11; 13:7.

[26] Lit., 'man.'

[27] Allusions to 'the robe of glory,' cf. S. P. Brock, "Baptismal Themes," p. 337 (n. 58).

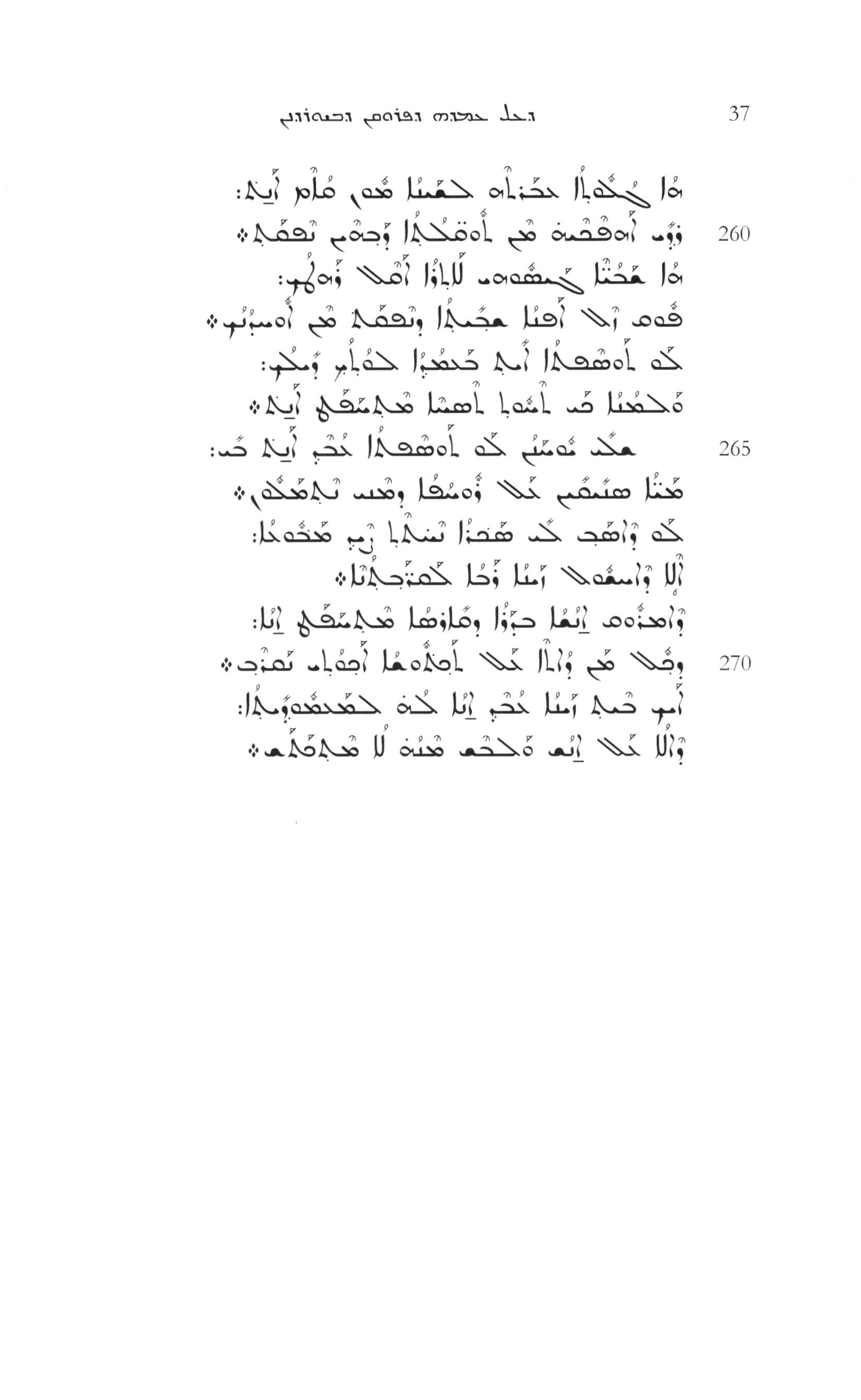

If I pass over and do not get baptized as you would withhold me,
no one will be able to take up the armour from the waters.
275 As a commander I took up the leadership in the contest
in order to be an example to the forces that are coming after me.
And if I turn aside from the road that I have taken hold of and come,
again those after me too will pass by, as they have seen me (doing).
And if they do not equip themselves with my power from the waters
280 they will not encounter the great battle as diligent ones.
While I do not need the furnace of the waters,[28] behold, I am entering[29]
so that humanity[30] that is worn out should be recast with that stamp of mine.[31]
I am stimulating them so that they should come to the fountain like me,
in order that with the coin[32] of mine they shall be stamped spiritually.

---

[28] 'furnace of waters,' cf. Bedjan I, p. 797; Narsai speaks of, 'spiritual furnace/crucible' *PO* 40, p. 106, 31 (tr. p. 107).

[29] Theodore of Mopsuestia, *On Baptism*: cf. A. Mingana (ed.), *Commentary of Theodore of Mopsuestia*, pp. 65–66.

[30] Lit., 'man.'

[31] Allusions to pre-baptismal anointing; cf. S. P. Brock, "Baptismal Themes," p. 337 (ns. 70, 72, metallurgical imagery → recasting the 'original stamp' and the 'image').

[32] Baptism and metallurgical imagery, cf. S. P. Brock, "Baptismal Themes," p. 337 (n. 71).

ܪܗܛ ܚܕܬܐ ܕܩܘܡܗ ܕܚܘܒܢܝ

أَي حُكَز إِنَا وَلَا حُضِم إِنَا أَمو وَبِكَمْلَس:
لَا إِنَه هُمصَس عُقَلا آَمَا هَم حَم هَمْنَا.
أَمو وَد مَللا نَحِبَا وَنَعًا حَلَا لَاحِمَهُمَا: 275
وَاهةَا وِقُدبِال حَمْنْكْدِبَال وَاَلَمِ حَلَمُوِب.
هَاٍ هَصطَا إِنَا هَنُه وَاوِزَنَا وِحَجِحَمِ هَالَمِ:
أَه هَنَه لَاوِد حَلَموِب حَجَنَمِ أَمو وَمَأَهب.
هَاٍ مَللا وَمِد لَا هَدِمَرَفَم هَم حَم هَمْنَا:
لَا أُونَم حَه حَمَاوِهَا وَحَا أَمو هَمَنْزَاٍ.   280
حَ لَا هِنَعِ إِنَا حَجُوَزا وِهَمْنَا هَا حَلَا إِنَا:
وَحَهَة لَحَلَا وَمِد نَحَنَعِقَمِ إِنَعَا وَحَحَه.
هِحَنَى إِنَا حَهَمِ وَاحَدبِ نَلَأَمِ زَى هَخَوِكَا:
وِحِقَدَنَبِلَا وَمِد نَحَلَحَنَمِ وَهِمَنَلَمِ.

285 To the tomb of water[33] I am bringing down humanity,
    so that I may make them immortal in the resurrection.
    I am making them enter into the moist womb[34] so
        that it will conceive them
    and give them the new birth without birth pangs.
    And again it is righteousness that I should be baptized
        by you, do not delay.
290 Come, open the road because the world is expecting
    to be renewed by me."

THE APPARENT IMPOSSIBILITY FOR JOHN TO BAPTIZE 'THE BAPTIZER OF ALL'

The feeble one approached the Powerful One and
    besought Him:
"Lord, how is it possible that this would happen?
To the bride of light who was betrothed to you I said
    this:
The Bridegroom, your Lord, will baptize with the   Matt 3:11; Mark 1:8; Luke 3:16
    Holy Spirit and fire."
295 Behold, she is looking to you that you may baptize her
    as I taught her,
and now how is it that she should approach to see
    that you are baptized by me?
I attested before her that I am not worthy, not even   Matt 3:11; Mark 1:8; Luke 3:16
    for your sandals;
and how shall I venture to place my hands upon your
    head?

---

[33] 'Tomb (*qabra*, grave) of water,' cf. S. P. Brock, "Baptismal Themes," p. 335 (n. 49). For other titles of Baptism in Jacob of Serugh, cf. "Baptismal Themes," p. 335, (n. 50). Water is an ambivalent symbol. It is at the same time destructive and constructive, death and life. Baptism is a 'death and resurrection' as well as 'new life' because water is the womb of many beings. Jacob employs both the Pauline vision of 'death and resurrection' and the Johannine vision of 'new life' regarding baptism. Narsai also uses this image, PO 40, pp. 86/87 (1. 273).

[34] Baptism = a womb: for other texts of Jacob of Serugh, see note 17 above. Narsai mentions the images of 'womb' and 'crucible' (*kura*) that moulds and renews human race: PO 40, p. 78 (lines 127–128, 143); p. 86 (1. 259); p. 88 (1. 295); p. 92 (1. 368); p. 106 (1. 31); Cf. A. Mingana (ed.), *Homiliae et Carmina*, Vol. I, p. 343,23.

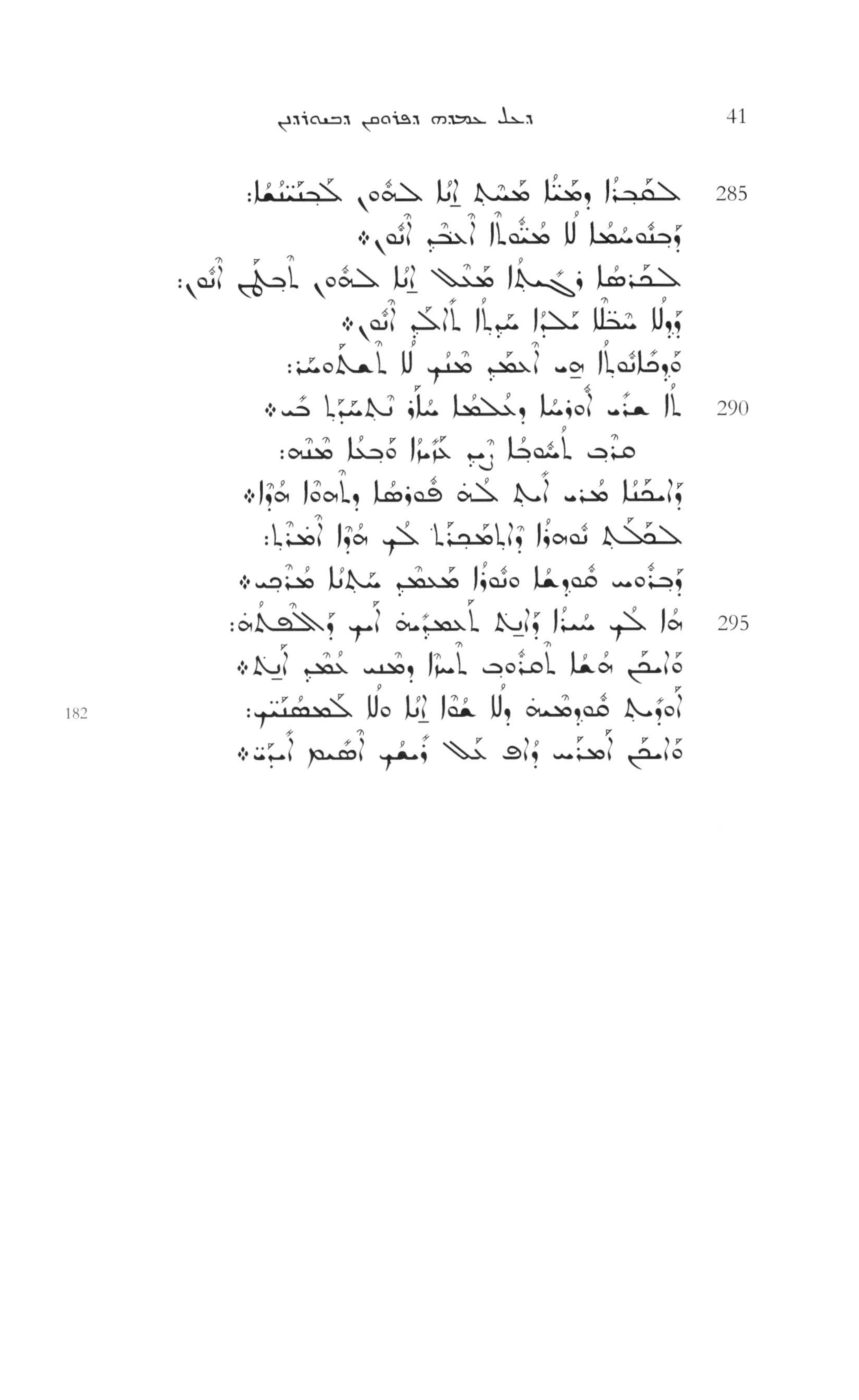

> In your name I have been baptizing her so that she shall be adorned by you;
> 300 and, O Holy One, in whose name shall I baptize you? I do not know.
> Behold, my word is the pledge to her and it is vigilant in her,
> because I had told her, "He will baptize you in the Holy Spirit."
> And now how shall I go back on my word and change my saying,
> and baptize you, O Baptizer of all, with water as (I did) to others?
> 305 I will turn out to be (guilty of) falsehood and you will be belittled
> and the bride will think that there is deficiency in her betrothed.
> What shall I say when I baptize the Forgiver of Debts,
> and with what expressions shall I observe the rite of baptism?
> Shall I baptize the Son in the name of the Father ! Behold, you are in His bosom
> 310 and there is not a breath of slightest gesture between you and Him.
> Shall I invoke the Son, You alone being the Sanctifier of Waters;
> and being holy, why should you wash your holiness in baptism?
> If you are baptized in the name of the Spirit, how is it possible
> that I shall sign the water separately because you are with the Spirit?
> 315 The Father is in His Son and the Son is wholly in His Father,
> and the Spirit who is from Him is one power without confusion.
> And how shall I, the poor one, perform this,
> and set a division in that undivided harmony?"

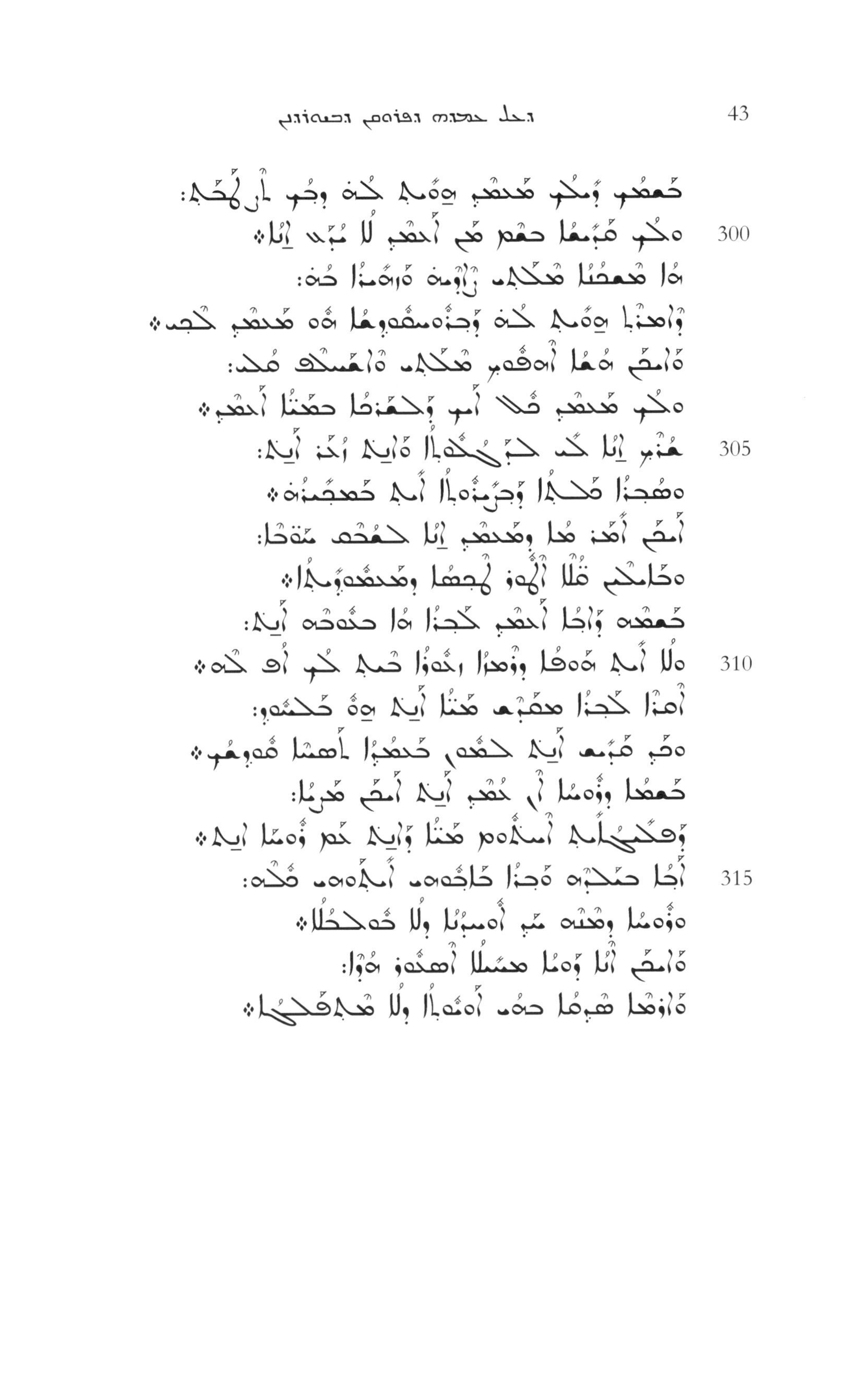

THE SON'S COMMAND TO JOHN AND THE BAPTISM OF THE HOLY ONE

"John, pass over from questions and be silent.
320   Now let there be to you no disputation here on account of these matters.
I have come to baptism, not because it should sanctify me,
nor is it necessary that you should say something when I am baptized.
Come silently, just place your hand on my head
and it belongs to the Father what to say about his Son.
325   Stretch out your right hand so that in appearance it may come to me,
and without any word of yours the Spirit will bear witness about the truth."

THE BAPTISM OF THE SON AND THE SANCTIFICATION OF THE WATERS

And while the son of barren parents was trembling on account of all this,
then he let the Son be baptized according to His wish.
He approached trembling, adored while confessing, reached Him while being shaken.
330   He was shaken and terrified but the power that would not fail him, supported him.
The Holy One came, and reached the waters to descend to be baptized,
and His fire kindled among the waves and inflamed them.[35]
The river leaped for joy in the pure womb of baptism,
just as John in Elizabeth towards his Lord.   Luke 1:44

---

[35] Rabbula Gospel has an illustration of Christ's Baptism in which the Jordan river is depicted in flames; See J. Leroy, *Les Manuscrits Syriaque a peintures* II, Paris 1964, p. 23 (on the left).

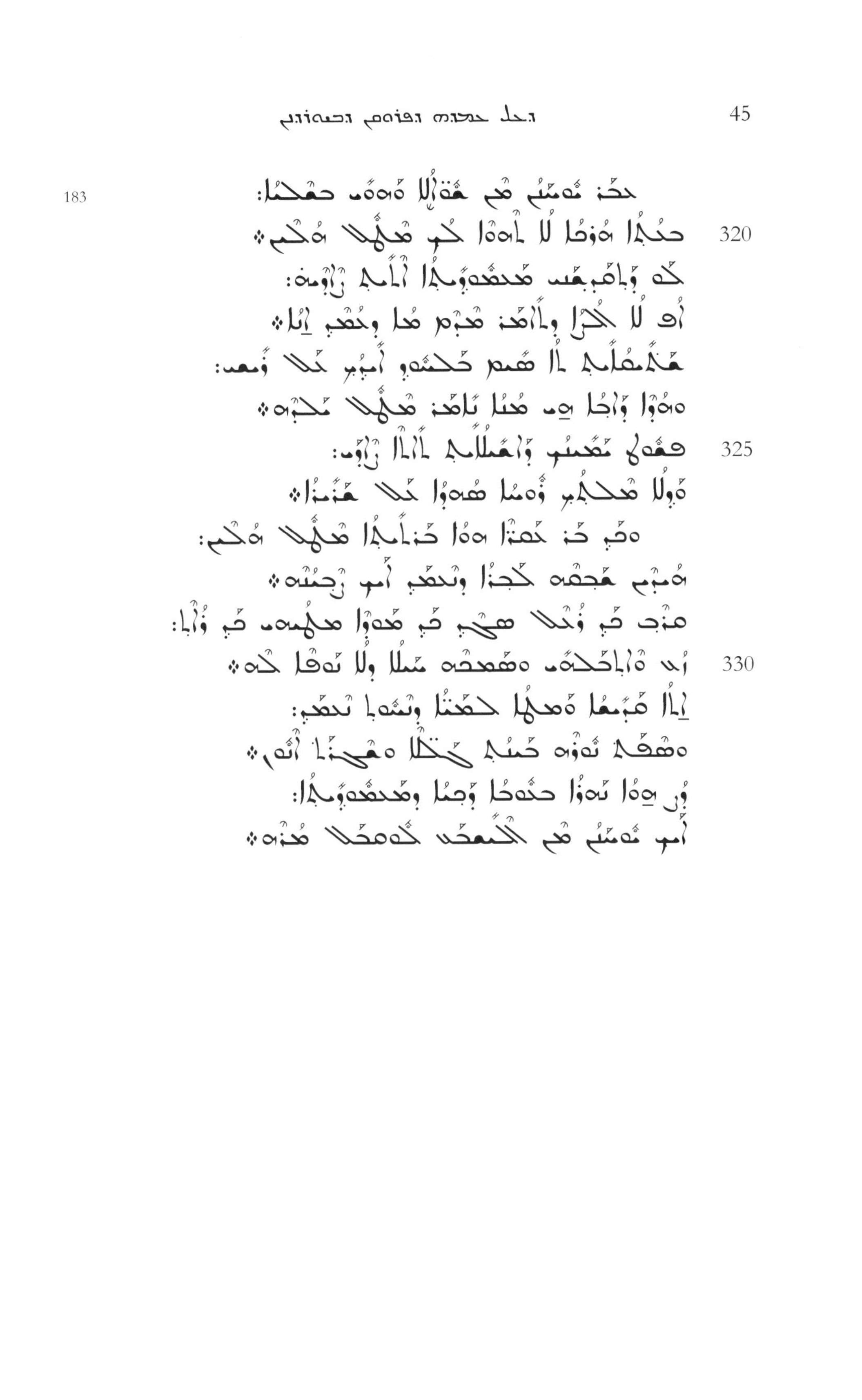

335 The waters were inflamed by the lightning of flames
because the Living Fire had come for baptism to be washed by them.
It *[the Living Fire]* sets the ages on fire and casts its flame into the fountain
and the glow from it kindled the river in holiness.
The ordinary water was mixed with the splendour of holiness,
340 because from the Holy One mercy had gone out and kindled it.
The Coal of Fire came down to be washed among the rushing streams   Isa 6:6[36]
and sprinkled there the fieriness of its holiness.
The Flame came and took off the garments that it was wearing
and descended to place fire in the waters of baptism.
345 The heavenly beings marvelled at that ablution of the Flame
when its glorious body was rinsed to sanctify the waters.
The rushing streams of water were mingled with rays of light
and the river had been set on fire with the brightness that dwelt in it.
The tips of the waves were tossed about by the currents
350 and the lightnings of flame surrounded it from all sides.
An amazement and a great wonder struck the creation
when the Flame descended to be baptized by John.
The whole air grew warm and became inflamed in a holy manner
because the Son of the Holy One descended for baptism though He was not lacking (anything).

---

[36] Christ = 'Coal of Fire,' cf. Ephrem, *Commentary on the Diatessaron*, I.25.

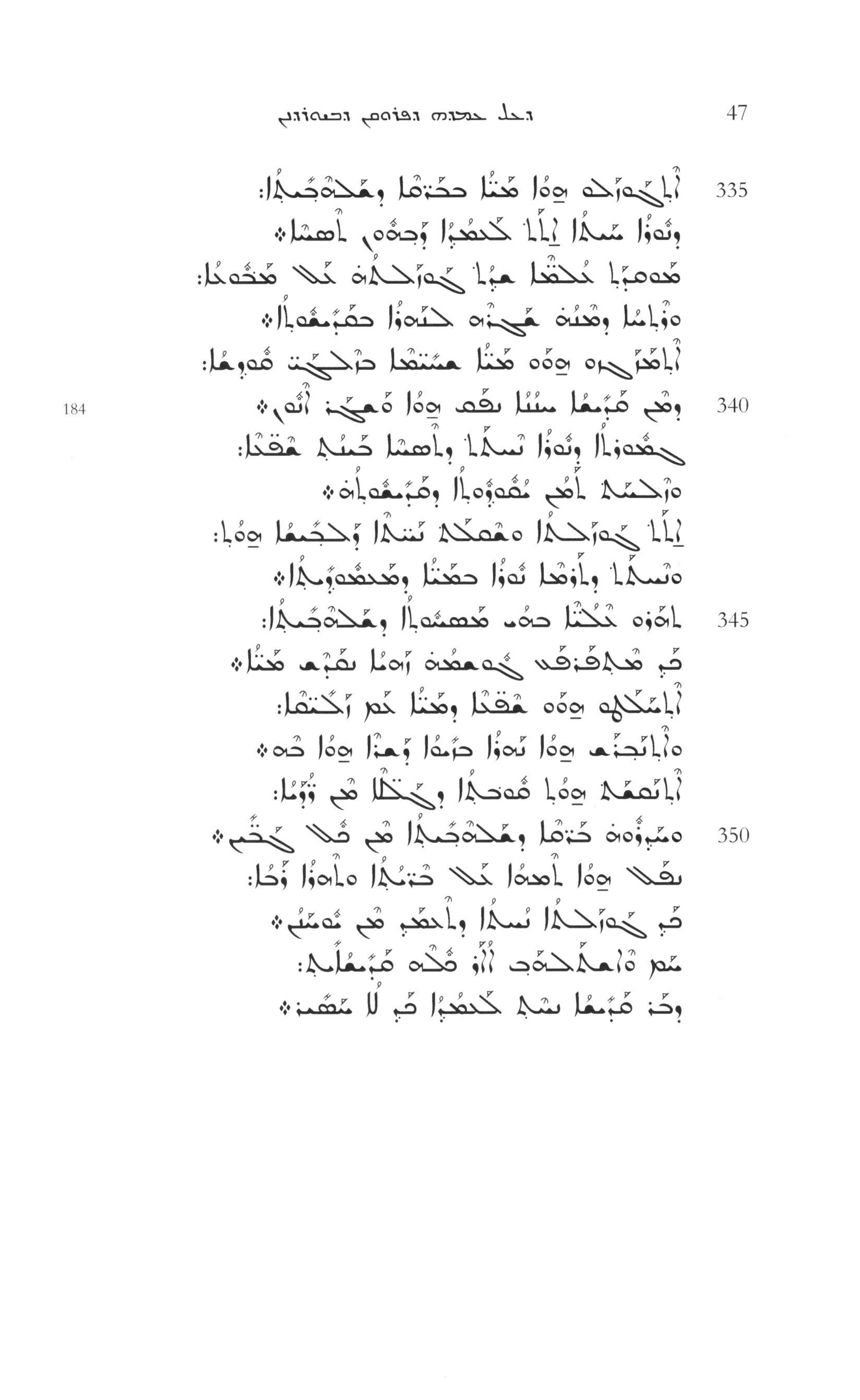

THE FATHER AND THE HOLY SPIRIT BEARING WITNESS UPON THE SON

355   The Spirit was present in the fire intensely
in order to receive the Bridegroom in splendour from within the waters.
Fair glory had been kindled from all regions,
and reverentially made solemn procession for the Son of the Kingdom.
Clouds of light floated from the extremities and stood still there,
360   to become a bridal chamber for the glorious Bridegroom to descend to be baptized.
Dark clouds issued forth, like veils of the royal palace,
so that when the Son of the King has been bathed, He could be received within them.
The Father stretched out chosen garments above the air;
Brightness and glory and flashes of astonishment as well as dark clouds.
365   He surrounded the river with amazing colours that were not apprehensible,
so that the marriage feast of the Only-Begotten Son should be exalted.
He rent the sky and raised His voice forcefully: Matt 3:17; Luke 3:22; Mark 1:11
"Behold, this is my Son; this is truly my Beloved."
The Spirit floated from the Father in a great wonder   Matt 3:16; Mark 1:10; Luke 3:22
370   and flew down, descended, rested upon and abode upon His Beloved.
She *[the Spirit]*[37] candidly came in the bodily form of a dove
to circle in the air there and to set up Her nest in the baptismal water.
She clothed Herself in the type of a dove, innocent among the flying creatures

---

[37] Here the Holy Spirit is feminine as usual in the early Syriac literature. Hence the later references to the Spirit in this homily are rendered feminine in the translation also.

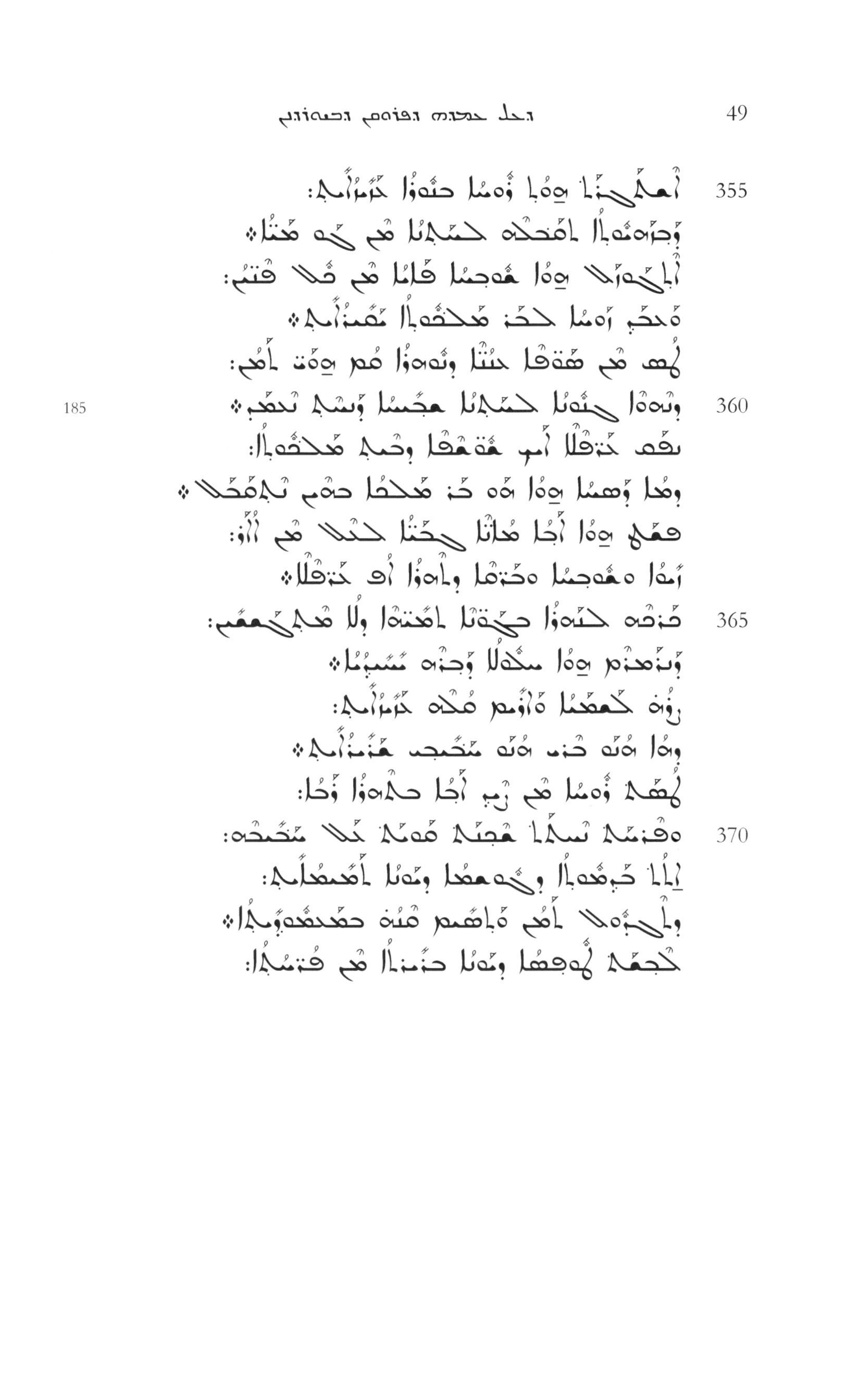

and she came to give witness to the True One in Her simplicity.
375 While She has been sent, She descended not to sanctify the Son
since the adorable Word did not need to sanctify His essence.
She did not besprinkle holiness by Her descent upon the Holy One;
She indeed gave witness[38] to the Redeemer when She appeared.
The Spirit became a finger for the Father and with it He showed,
380 "This is my Son, you should not be in doubt about His advent."
Had not the Spirit descended upon the True One
who would have known where the voice of the Father would rest?
Together with that word which was proclaimed by the Supreme One,
as with a finger the Spirit showed that this is the King.
385 For if She *[the Spirit]* had not rested upon Him specifically
the voice would have roamed over many among the crowds.
Behold, they would have heard the voice which said, "This is my Beloved One,"
and they would have asked in doubt about whom it spoke.
The Spirit descended to rest upon Him in a holy manner
390 not because holiness was insufficient in Him, and it had to be made perfect in Him.
The Law too of its own accord summons two witnesses — Deut 19:15
because someone alone would not be accepted, even when he is true.

---

[38] Cf. Ephrem, *Commentary on the Diatessaron*, IV 3.

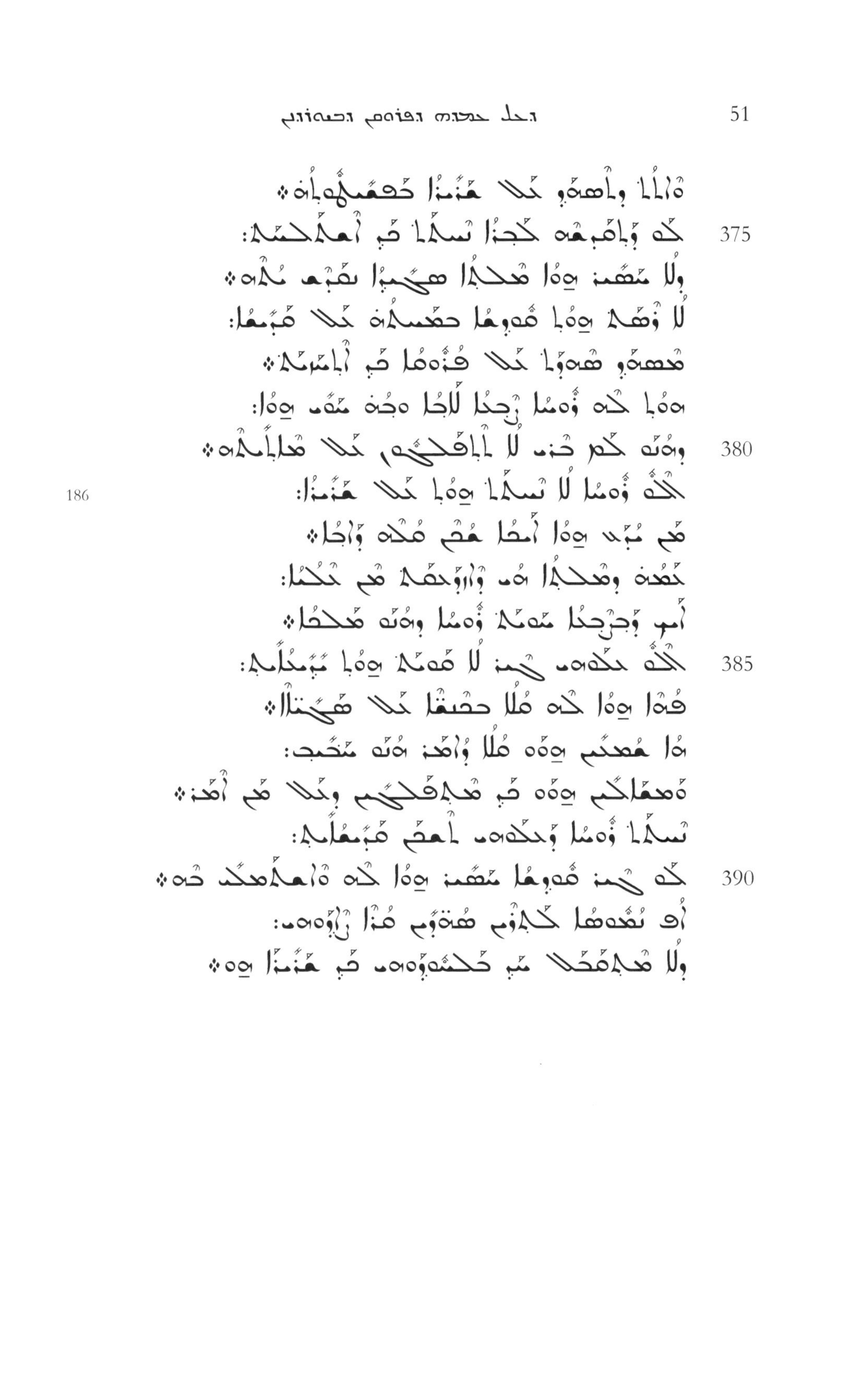

The Father and the Spirit together bore witness to the Only-Begotten,
so that legally they might give what is due to the same True One.
395 The voice of the Father and the Holy Spirit descended simultaneously,
so that no one should reject their testimony when She appeared.
The voice of the Father tore asunder the sky and went out from it
and there stood over the river a sea of boundless light,
The Spirit with its wings carried and brought a great glory
400 and the desert overflowed with the brightness which was poured forth from the Most High.

THE BRIDE'S RECOGNITION OF THE ROYAL BRIDEGROOM

The Church, the bride of light, marvelled at the Royal Bridegroom,
because through His washing the height and the depth were reconciled.
She saw the river entirely aflame, with its rushing streams trembling
and she heard the voice of the Father that proclaimed about His beloved One.
405 She sent for and called that Harp of the Spirit, David,
to come to sing the songs that are suitable for the marriage feast.
"Come, son of Jesse and bring with you your hymns — Ruth 4:17,22; 1 Sam 16
so that today, on the marriage feast of your Lord and your son, we may rejoice.
Make your tones sing out clearly and stretch out the strings of your harp,
410 and set forth hymns that will make clear and cause me to rejoice.
Do not tell me hintingly when you are singing,
make clear your word and let truth resound in your hymn.
Reveal, and explain to me, on what account does the river tremble,

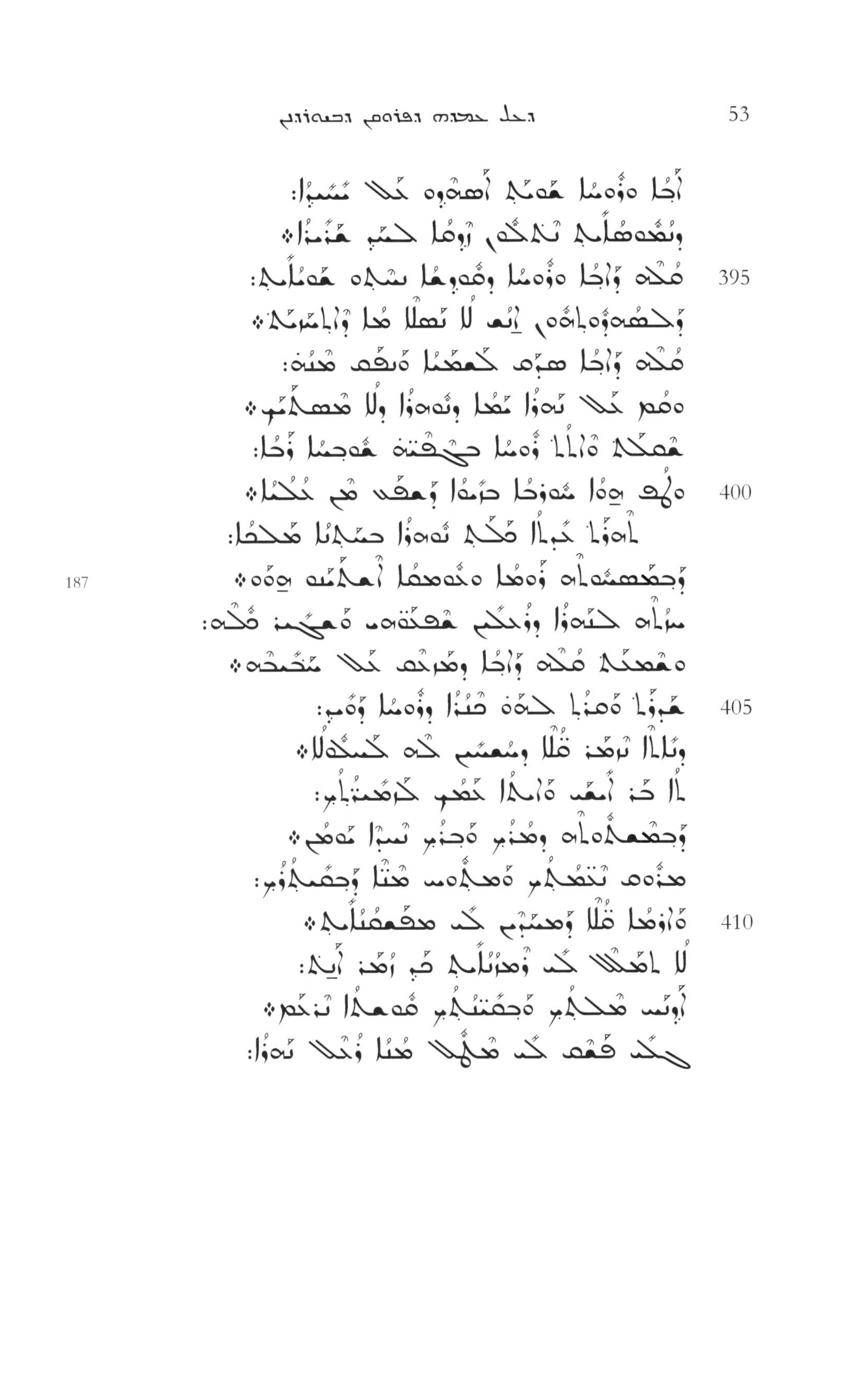

and what force compelled the depth and it trembled
    and became dismayed?
415 What is the voice that, behold, descends from the
    height to the depth,
and for what purpose are these continuous lightnings
    that have inflamed the air?"
David laid out hymns of praise in response to the
    Bridegroom
so as to explain the matter to the Church as it was.
"The waters have truly seen you, God, and they
    feared:
420 The abysses too trembled and the clouds of the air   Ps 77:16–17
    sprinkled water.
The whole nature of the waters perceived that you
    have visited *them*.
Seas, abysses, rivers, springs and pools.
They thronged each other to be blessed by your foot
    steps
because your great manifestation that came upon
    them caused them to tremble.
425 You stepped upon Jordan as upon the summit of all
    seas;
and the extremities of the abysses and of the floods
    trembled at your power.
The whole nature of the waters was stirred by your
    descent,
because by your baptism you made everyone worthy
    of pardon.
The waters of seas, although distant, are not distant
430 because the power of your holiness has stirred mysti-
    cally and visited them.
For this reason the waters truly saw you and they   Ps 77:16
    feared.
Even the abysses trembled because by your descent
    you have caused them to tremble.
Clouds sprinkled water into the river when you were
    baptized
so that they too should not be deprived of your de-
    scent.

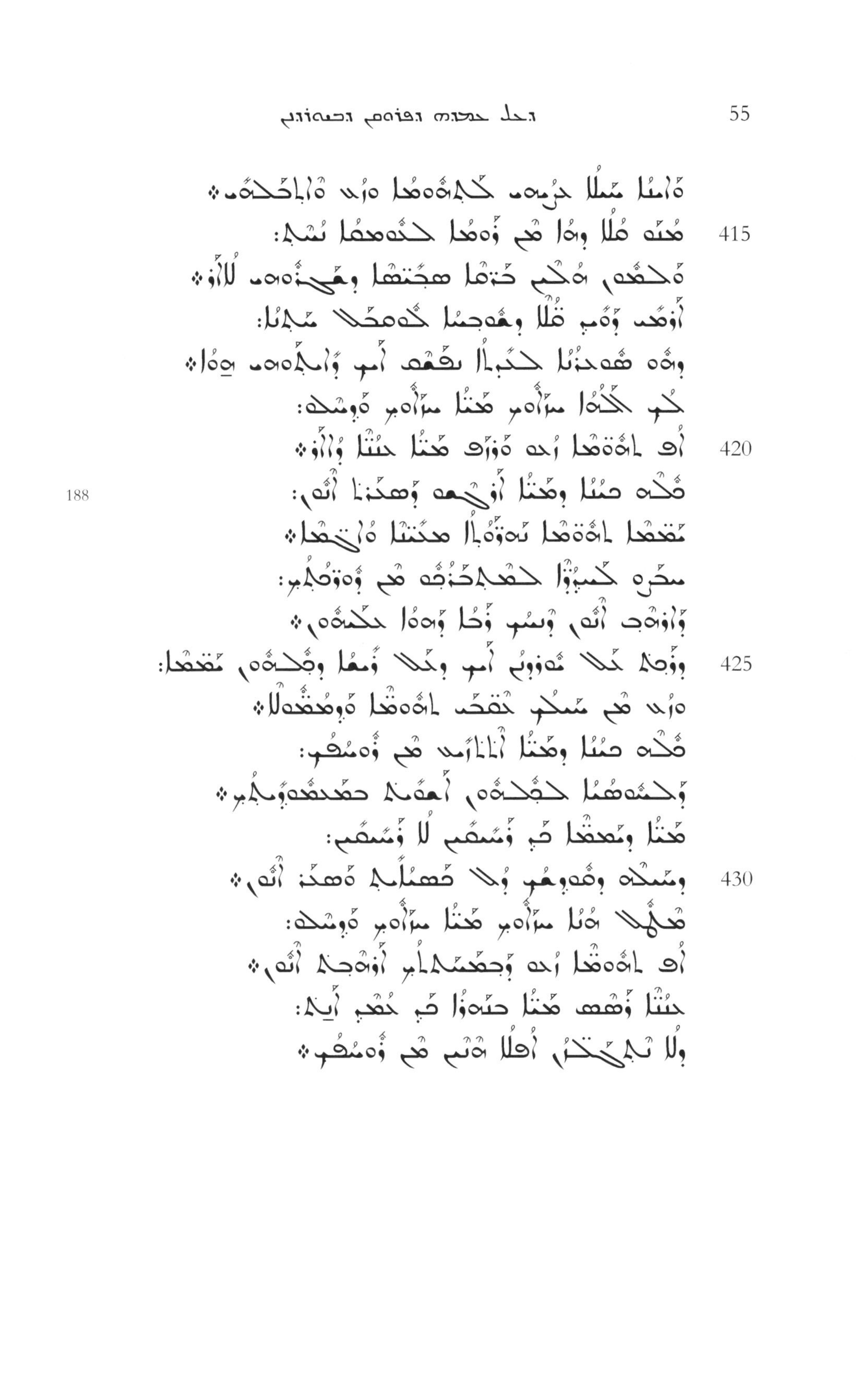

435	Behold, even the heights of heaven proclaimed again through your heavenly Father,
	so that in His testimony the earth should perceive that you are the Only-Begotten.
	Your lightnings illumined the earth and it saw the glorious Light.
	The earth was troubled by darkness until you came.
	Waters saw you and they feared you as the Lord.
440	The breath of your energy heated them while you were descending."
	David explained the cause of the matter when he sang,
	and Zechariah came; he stimulated the Church to show her,
	"This is the One whose name, I had told you, is Day-Star.[39]
	Behold, he has shone forth and the extremities were enlightened by his rays."

THE BAPTISM OF JESUS AND THE PROCLAMATION OF THE FATHER

445	John came near and stretched out his hand upon the Flame
	and the ranks of watchers took shelter among one another out of fear.
	The hosts marvelled at the wonder that they saw
	while the dry-stick took hold of the Coal of Fire, but was not scorched by it. *Isa 6:6*
	The heavenly beings marvelled at the fearful sign that took place there
450	because the fleshly hand was not harmed by the Flame.
	Seraphs cover their faces before His flame *Isa 6:2*
	but a hand fashioned out of clay is placed upon His head.
	A brick moulded from the soil laid hold of the Sea,

---

[39] Denha, Cf. Zech 6:12 (Peshitta); Luke 1:78.

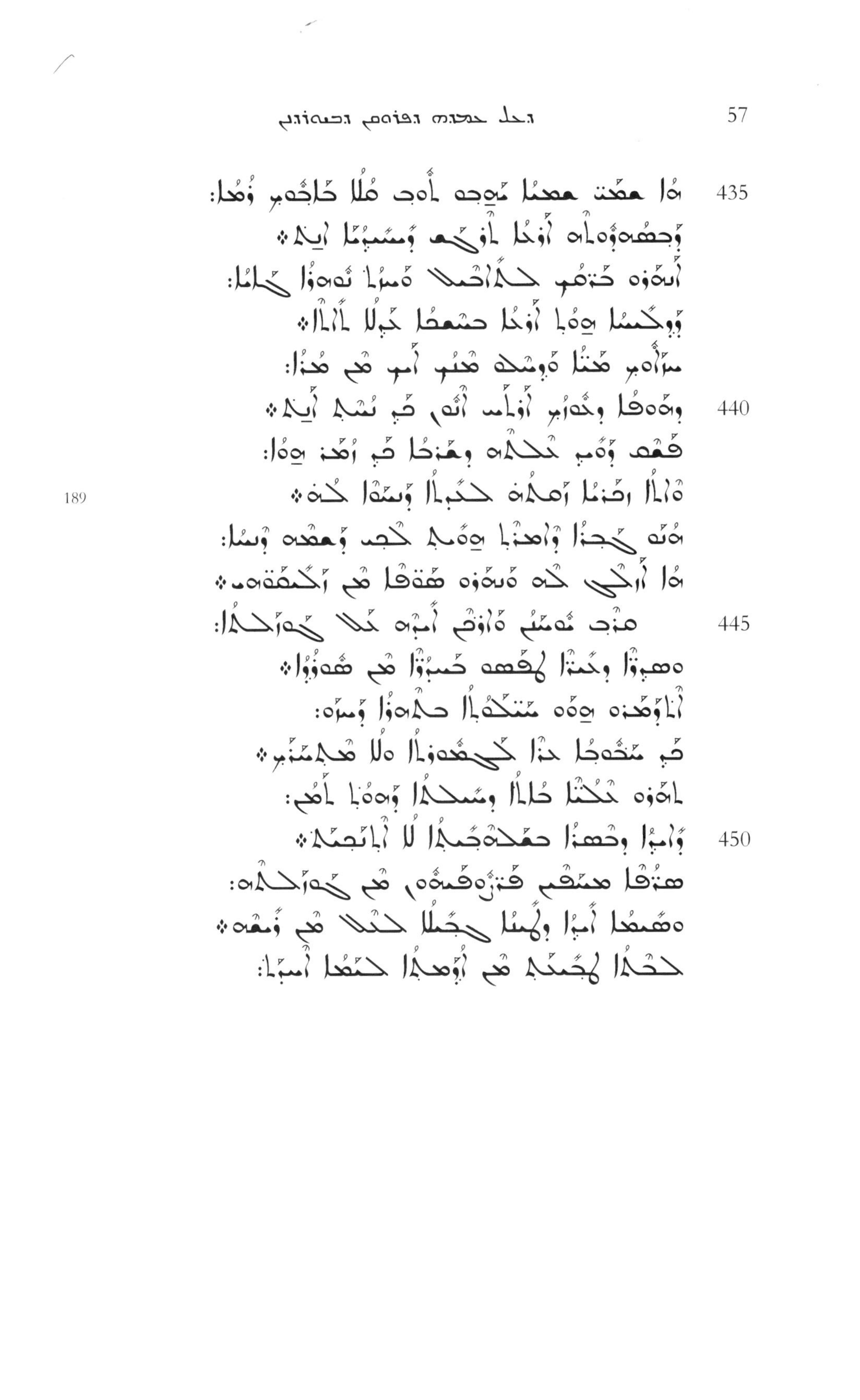

and set its hand upon the Flood but it did not dissolve.
455 It is a marvel, to say: While the fiery beings were powerless before Him,
yet He descended beneath the right hand of the son of a barren woman for baptism.
Carried by the cherubs, glorious on the chariot, veiled from the watchers,
He was hidden from the ranks, glorified among the gatherings, awesome over the legions.
The orders remain veiled, the gatherings are perplexed, the ranks tremble;
460 The forces quake, choirs are shaken, the thousands shudder.
The flame stood aside trembling
as He descended to be baptized by the dust that His hands had fashioned.
Heaven was torn open and the Father proclaimed about His Beloved.
The Spirit shone forth and stood there to bear witness concerning the Only-Begotten.
465 The voice proceeded from the inner-chamber of the royal palace,
So that it might declare about the Son of the King that He is not a stranger.
The hidden utterance was set in motion not by the mouth
to come out to give witness concerning that Offspring of the divinity.
That Word hidden from all had been revealed
470 when it called out over that Hidden One who had come to manifestation.
A loud voice resounded in the sky without a tongue,
from the One without body, over His Beloved who had become embodied.
He did not speak through an angel at that moment
nor did He announce through the glowing mouth of any of the watchers.
475 He did not borrow for himself any word or voice from the heavenly beings

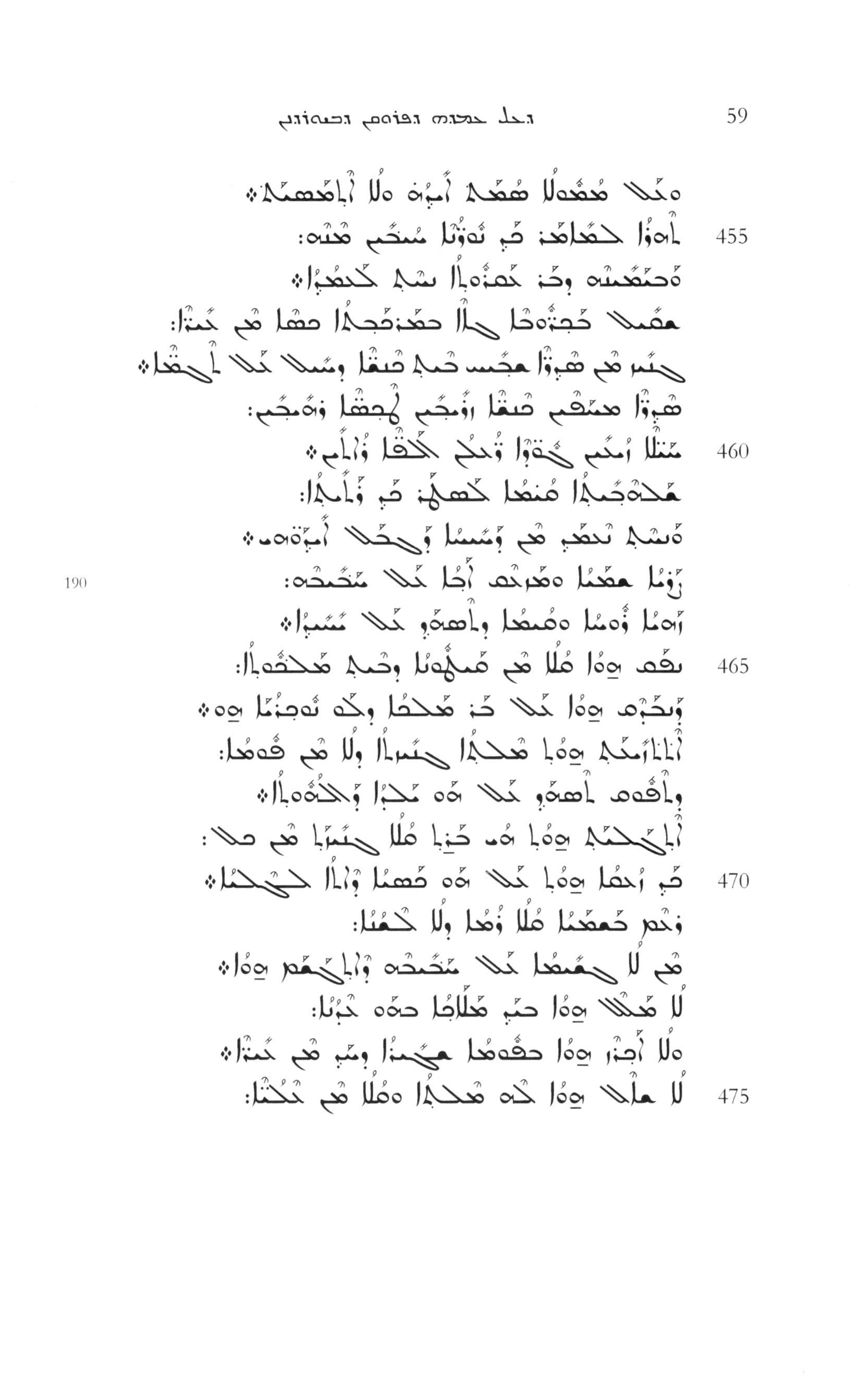

because He spoke from His essence about His Only-Begotten.
The Father himself truly spoke personally
so as to indicate that His Son was genuine.
A new word was heard among the gatherings,
480   the exalted voice, the like of which was not again spoken,
A melody that had never been sown in the ears of men,
A fearful resonance that by itself made its voice heard.
He did not speak like that word at any (other) time,
because He did not have another son in any other place.
485   The Mighty One thundered to express His love for His Son among the crowds
to announce to them that He has a true son.
The affection of the Fatherhood was greatly stirred towards the Only-Begotten,
and it *[the Fatherhood]* had uttered to show that He was his Beloved.
The divinity exalted above all was not ashamed
490   to see His Son clothed in a body and baptized in the water.
That Majesty did not diminish when its Beloved One
descended for baptism that was employed for redemption.
It was not any insufficiency of His that was filled up from the water
so that the Father might renounce and not acknowledge Him because He was deficient.
495   He was perfect before He descended as well as after the descent,
and the Father had the confidence to acknowledge His Son.

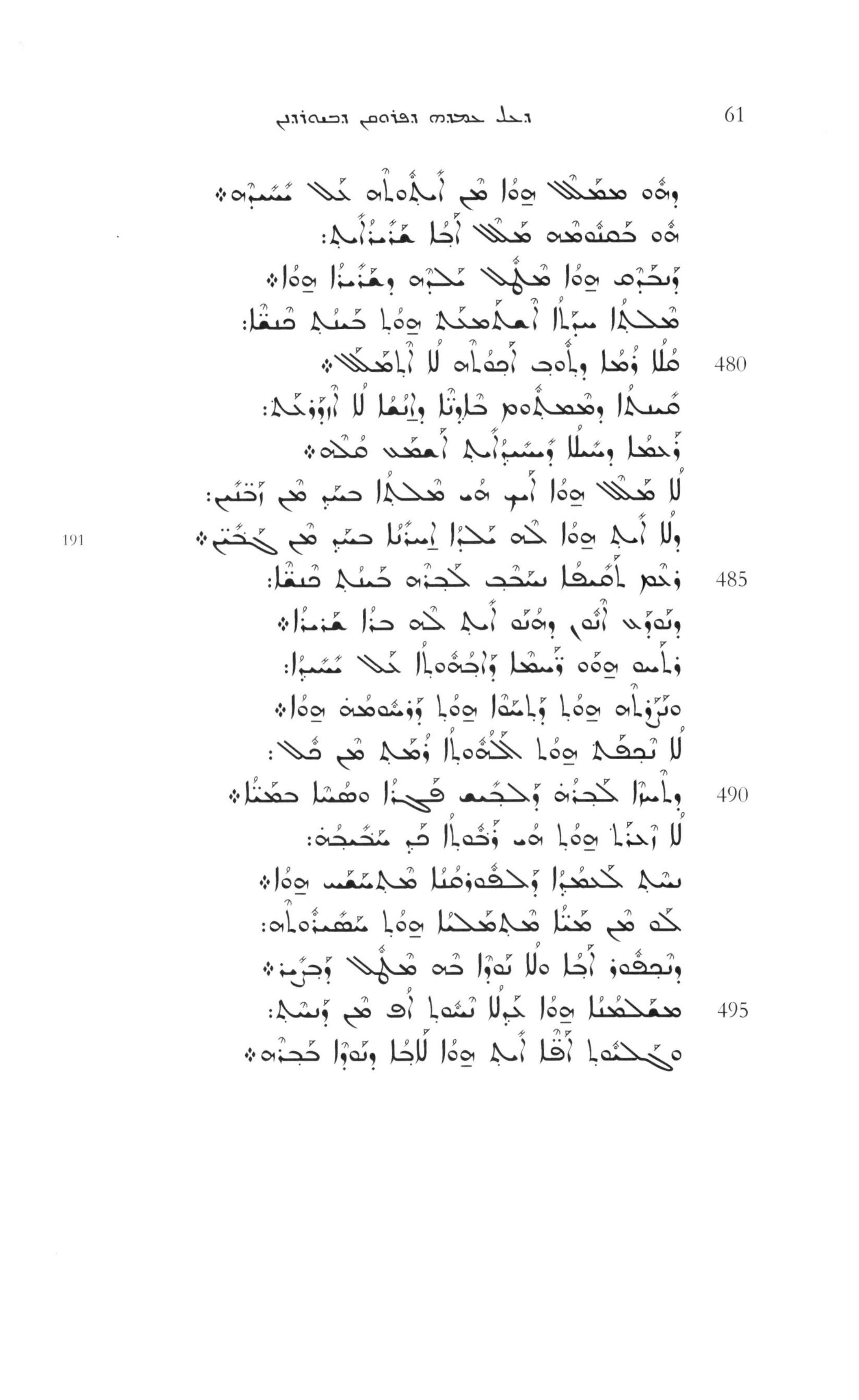

و

THE FLOWING OF PRIESTHOOD, KINGSHIP AND HOLINESS INTO CHRIST

This is the reason that called Him to come for baptism;
so that the dominion of the priests[40] should be concluded in Him and it should proceed from Him.
The Father gave the deposit to Moses on the mountain   Exod 29:9; 40:15
500 and sent His Son who received it from John in the water.
It was handed down by the tribe of Levi,   Num 16:10
and the Lion's Whelp of the house of Judah arose and   Gen 49:9
carried it from him [*John*].[41]
Holiness overflowed upon mount Sinai from the Exalted One,
and through John it overflowed upon our Redeemer.
505 From His very beginning our Lord took it upon himself to accomplish His way,
so as not to join any other path as an alien one.[42]
That priesthood which had been handed down from   Exod 28:3; 29:9
the house of Aaron
proceeded from our Redeemer through the apostles to the world.[43]
Not because He was lacking in the great priesthood of the priests

---

[40] Cf. Bedjan IV, p. 781, the Priesthood of the house of Aaron has been received by Christ from John; S. P. Brock, "Baptismal Themes," p. 329 (n. 18); see also *HNat* 4:210.

[41] The transmission of Jewish Priesthood on Christ' in Aphrahat and Ephrem: *Dem* XXI, 13; Ephrem's prose homily 'On Our Lord,' 53, 54; *HcHaer* 22:19; cf. E. J. Duncan, *Baptism in the Demonstrations of Aphraates*, p. 105; R. Murray, *Symbols of Church and Kingdom*, pp. 178–181; S. P. Brock, "Baptismal Themes," p. 329 (n. 19).

[42] 'joining an alien path' might be alluding to Adam's journey on an alien path after his alienation from God. It might equally be an echo of anti-Marcionite and anti-Jewish pattern of discourses.

[43] Aphrahat: *Dem* XXI 13 = PS I/964; XXIII 20 = PS II/65; Ephrem: *HcHaer* 22:19; 24:22–23; R. Murray, *Symbols of Church and Kingdom*, pp. 55, 178–82; "Mary, the Second Eve," p. 374; R. Murray, in *The Christian Priesthood*, (ed.) N. Lash and J. Rhymer, pp. 33–34.

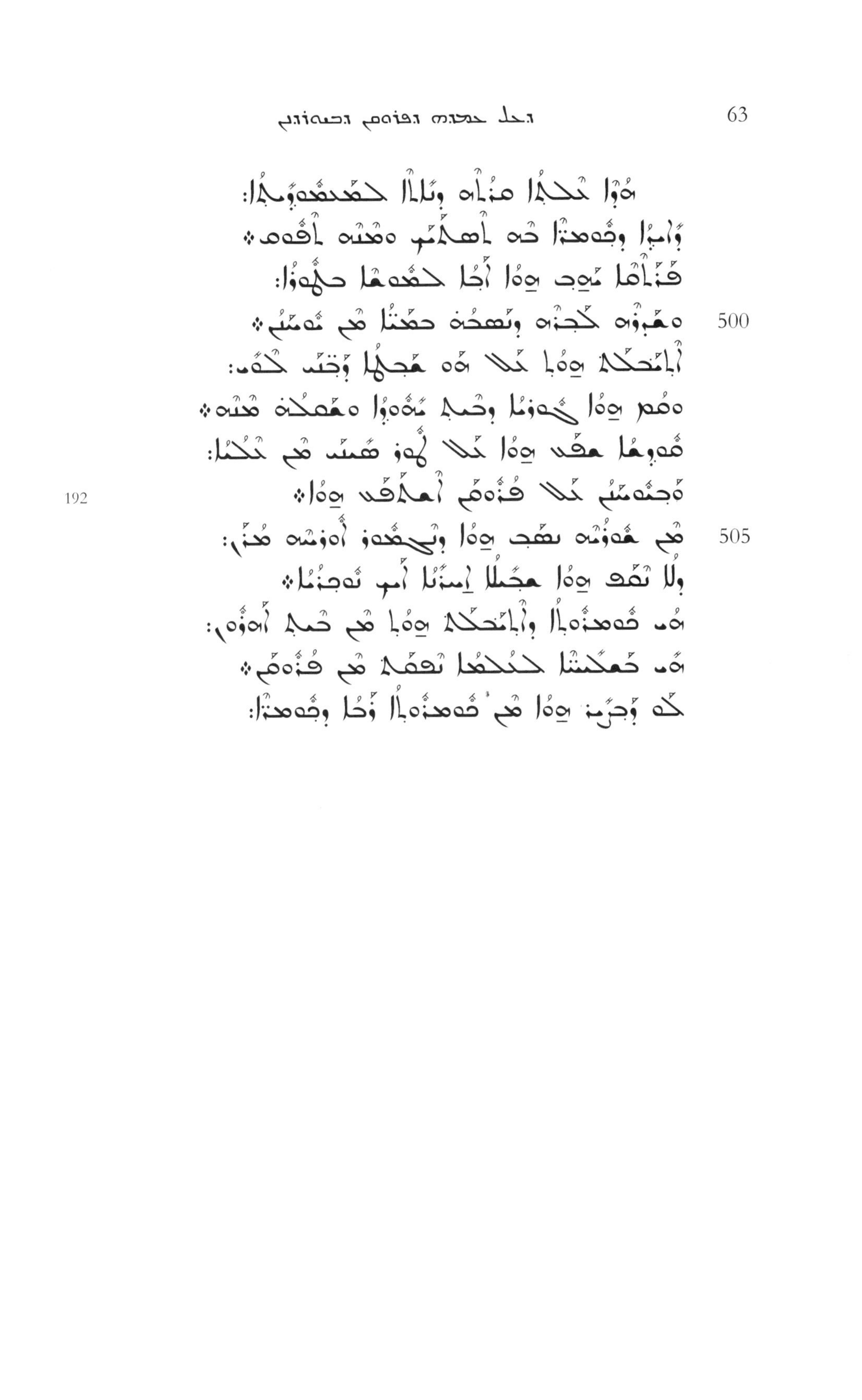

510   did He receive it at Baptism and then gave it:
> It was so as not to confound the path of truth which His Father has trodden out,
> from what belonged to Him did He make the renewal of old things.[44]
> It is not because the ocean is lacking in fullness
> that all streams and rivers flow towards it.

515   By nature water hurries to the sea while it [the sea] does not lack;
> and the whole sea is not made to abound more than it already is.[45]
> It is not because He lacked that Christ received the hand of (the priesthood of) Aaron
> nor was it because He lacked (anything) that He received the kingdom from the house of David.
> The kingdom proceeded with the priesthood and rested upon Him,

520   while He is the High Priest and the King of kings.
> Holiness overflowed and came and fell upon Him
> as a brooklet into the full ocean which did not lack anything.
> The kingdom came from the house of David and poured out upon Him
> While His kingdom is much richer than the sea.

525   He ascended as He descended in a holy manner, as He is
> and He was received on the wing of the voice from His Begetter.
> The Spirit encircled the baptized Bridegroom with feathers of glory
> and the Church became confirmed that it is He and she fell down before Him.

---

[44] *HNat* 4: 204–214.

[45] Cf. *HVirg* 8:7–15 where Ephrem equates Christ with the sea (Stanza no. 12) into which all streams of types, symbols and parables flow. Ephrem speaks of Christ as the Lord of symbols in *HVirg* 6:7; *HcHaer* 22:19; R. Murray, *Symbols of Church and Kingdom*, p. 179.

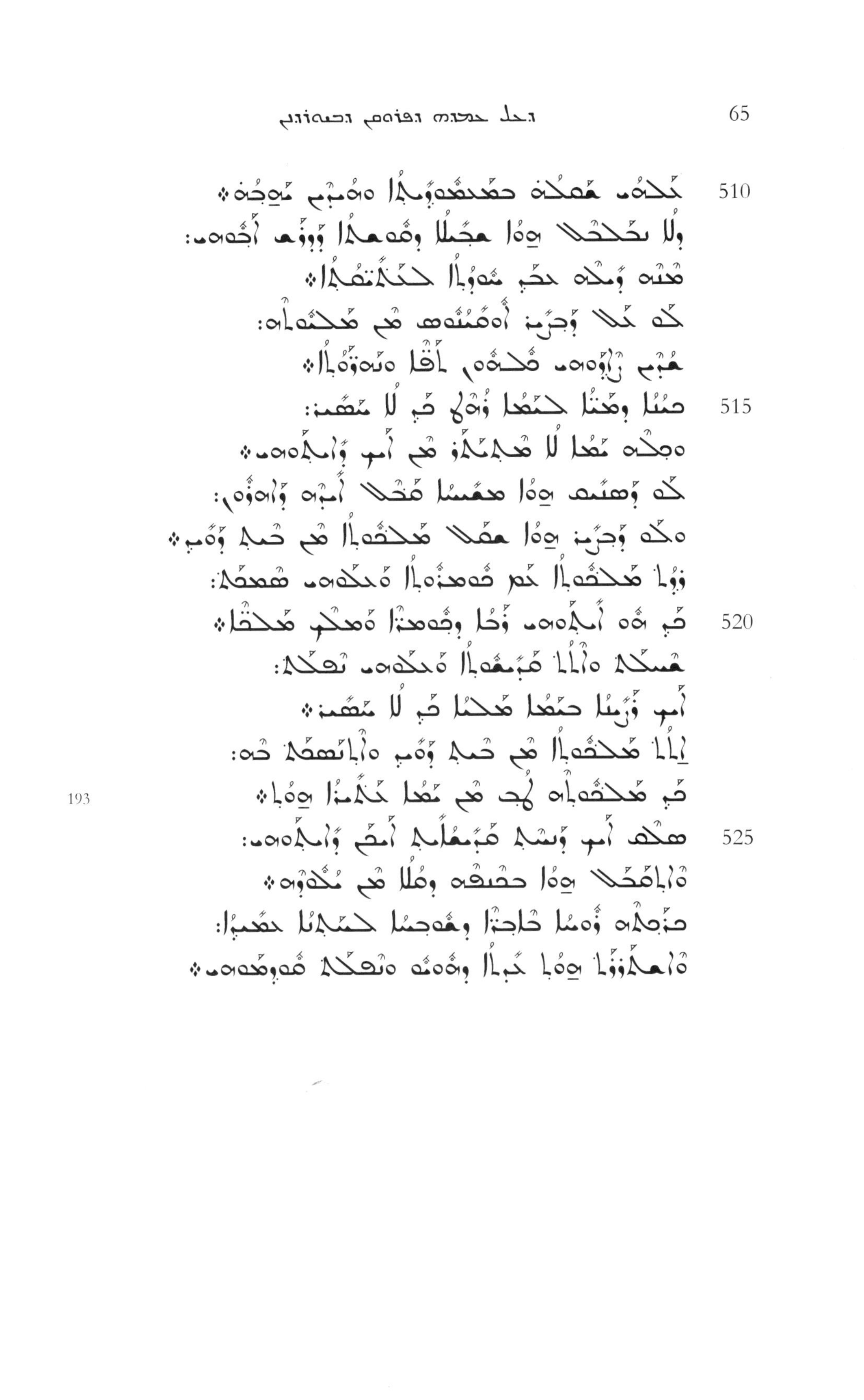

O Perfect One, who came so that he might perfect the insufficient by the waters;
530 let your great mercy overflow from you upon my insufficiency.
Blessed is He who came and was baptized by His envoy as it pleased Him.
He is the one who sanctified baptism; To Him be glory.

End of the homily on the baptism of Our Redeemer from John.

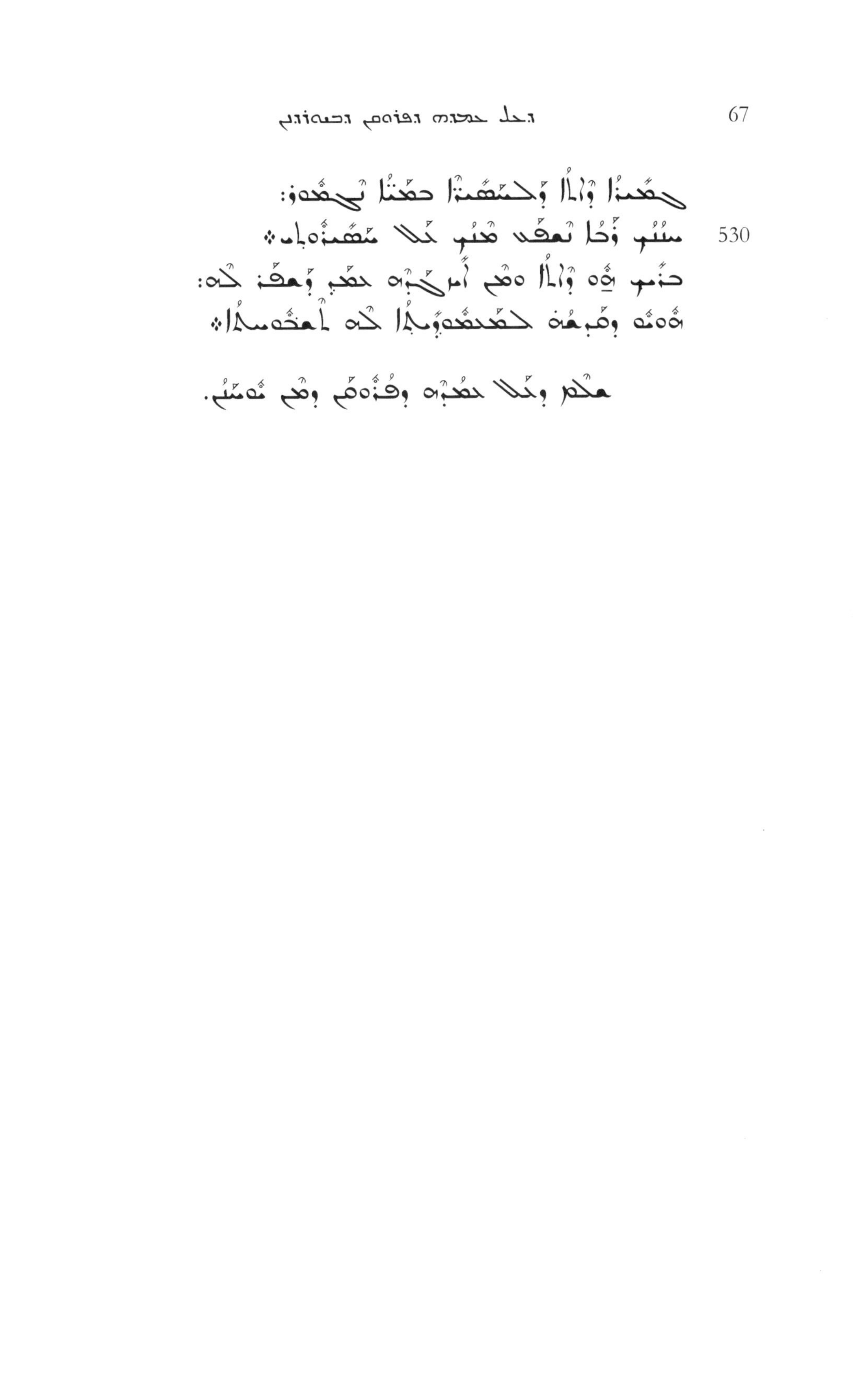

BIBLIOGRAPHY OF WORKS CITED

(A) SYRIAC AUTHORS

Aphrahat, *Demonstrations* (ed. J. Parisot, Patrologia Syriaca I.1–2; Paris, 1894, 1907); English tr. K. Valavanolickal, *Aphrahat, Demonstrations*, I-II (Moran Etho 23–4; 2005).

Ephrem, *HAzym* = *Hymni de Azymis*, in *Des heiligen Ephraem des Syrers Paschahymnen* (ed. E. Beck, CSCO 248–9 = Scr. Syri 108–9; 1964).

_____, *HFid* = *Des heiligen Ephraem des Syrers Hymnen de Fide* (ed. E. Beck, CSCO 154–5 = Scr/ Syri 73–4; 1955).

_____, *HcHaer* = *Des heiligen Ephraem des Syrers Hymnen contra Haereses* (ed. E. Beck, CSCO 169–70 = Scr. Syri 76–7; 1957).

_____, *HNat* = *Des heiligen Ephraem des Syrers Hymnen de Nativitate (Epiphania)* (ed. E. Beck, CSCO 186–7 = Scr. Syri 82–3; 1959).

_____, *HVirg* = *Des heiligen Ephraem des Syrers Hymnen de Virginitate* (ed. E. Beck, CSCO 223–4 = Scr. Syri 94–5; 1962).

_____, *SdDN* = *Des heiligen Ephraem des Syrers Sermo de Domino nostro* (ed. E. Beck, CSCO 270–1 = Scr. Syri 116–7; 1966).

_____, L. Leloir, *Saint Éphrem. Commentaire de l'Évangile Concordant* (Chester Beatty Monographs 8; Dublin, 1963).

Jacob of Sarug = *Homiliae Selectae Mar-Jacobi Sarugensis* I–V (ed. P. Bedjan; Paris/Leipzig, 1905–10; repr. ed. S. P. Brock; Piscataway, 2006, with extra volume VI).

_____, *Jacques de Sarug. Homélies contre les juifs* (ed. M. Albert; PO 38.1; 1978).

_____, *Jacques de Saroug. Quatre homélies métriques sur la Création* (ed. Kh. Alwan; CSCO 508–9 = Scr. Syri 214–5; 1989).

Narsai, = *Narsai doctoris Syri Homiliae et Carmina*, I–II (ed. A. Mingana; Mosul, 1905).

_____, *Narsai's Metrical Homilies on the Nativity, Epiphany, Passion, Resurrection and Ascension* (ed. F. G. McLeod; PO 40.1; 1979).

_____, *The Liturgical Homilies of Narsai* (tr. R. H. Connolly; Texts and Studies 8:1; 1909).

Theodore of Mopsuestia, *Commentary on Baptism* (ed. and tr. A. Mingana, Woodbrooke Studies 6; Cambridge, 1933).

(B) MODERN WORKS

T. Bou Mansour, *La théologie de Jacques de Saroug*, I (Kaslik, 1993).

S. P. Brock, "Baptismal themes in the writings of Jacob of Serugh," in Symposium Syriacum (OCA 205; 1978), 325–47.

_____, "Some important baptismal themes in the Syriac tradition," *Harp* 4 (1991), 189–214.

_____, *Syriac Perspectives on Late Antiquity* (London, 1984).

_____, *The Luminous Eye. The Spiritual World Vision of St Ephrem* (2nd edn, Kalamazoo, 1992).

E. J. Duncan, *Baptism in the Demonstrations of Aphraates the Persian Sage* (Washington, 1945).

Holy Transfiguration Monastery, "A Homily on that which our Lord said in the Gospel that the Kingdom of Heaven is like unto Leaven...," *The True Vine* 3 (1989), 44–57.

R. Graffin, "Recherches sur le thème de l'Église épouse," *L'Orient Syrien* 3 (1958), 317–36.

J. Leroy, *Les manuscrits syriaques à peintures*, I–II (Paris, 1964).

J-J. P. Martin, "Discours de Jacques de Saroug sur la chute des idoles," *Zeitschrift der deutschen morgenländischen Gesellschaft* 29 (1876), 107–47.

R. Murray, "Christianity's 'Yes' to Priesthood," in N. Lash and J. Rhymer (eds), *The Christian Priesthood* (9th Downside Symposium, 1970), 17–43.

_____, *Symbols of Church and Kingdom. A Study in Early Syriac Tradition* (Cambridge, 1975; revised edn Piscataway NJ, 2004).

INDEX OF NAMES AND THEMES

Aaron, 507, 517
Adam, 203–3, 208, 210
afflicted, 3
authority, 188, 189
Bridegroom, 1, 28, 30, 52, 62, 68, 82, 85, 106, 110, 111, 116, 126, 130, 132, 135, 152, 158, 163, 178, 294, 356, 360, 401, 417, 527
captivity, 256, 259, 260, 262
David, 144, 172, 177, 405, 441, 518, 523
defilement, 14
desire, 204, 209
dishonour, 221
Elizabeth, 3, 48
fear, 446
forgiveness, 134, 193, 194
fornication, 10
holiness, 134, 148, 197, 312, 338, 339, 342, 377, 390, 430, 503, 521
Holy Spirit, 139, 294, 302, 395
honour, 219
Isaiah, 31
Jesse, 407

Jesus, 114
John the Baptist, 19, 51, 81, 89, 115, 182, 237, 265, 319, 334, 445, 500, 504
Jordan, 425
kingship, 196
leadership, 275
Levi, 501
love, 114, 485
Mary, 231
mercy, 215, 216, 340, 530
Messiah, 64, 80
Moses, 499
mystery, 52, 91
Nazirite, 71
persecuted, 5
poverty, 40
priesthood, 195, 198, 507, 509, 517, 519
resurrection, 286
Sacrificial lamb, 156
sanctification, 10, 266
Sinai, 503
Zechariah, 442

INDEX OF BIBLICAL REFERENCES

Gen
  1:26   203
  49:9   502
Exod
  28:3   507
  29:9   499, 507
  40:15   499
Num
  16:10   501
Lev
  16:20–31   156
Jud
  7:1–4   9
Ruth
  4:17, 22   407
1 Sam
  16   407
  16:1–13   144
Ps
  45:10   174
  77:16   420, 431
  77:17   420
Isa
  1:27   37
  6:2   451
  6:6   341, 448
  40:3   46, 53
Hos
  2:19, 20   3
Zech
  6:12   443

  13:1   4
Matt
  3:2   27
  3:11   69, 74, 113, 294, 297, 370
  3:14   184
  3:17   104, 368
  22:2–14   1
Mark
  1:7   69
  1:8   294, 297
  1:10   370
  1:11   104, 368
Luke
  1:44   334
  1:78   443
  3:15   80, 135
  3:16   69, 74, 113, 294, 297
  3:22   111, 368, 370
  14:16–24   1
John
  1:26   111
  1:29   166
  1:33   91, 102
  1:34   102
2 Cor
  11:2   3
Col
  2:9   199
Titus
  3:4   213